The Grapes of Wrath

BARRON'S SIMPLIFIED APPROACH

TO
The Grapes of Wrath
JOHN STEINBECK

By Robert L. Gale
ENGLISH DEPARTMENT
UNIVERSITY OF PITTSBURGH

BARRON'S EDUCATIONAL SERIES, INC.

WOODBURY, NEW YORK

TO MAUREEN

ACKNOWLEDGMENTS

The author and the publisher of *Barron's Simplified Approach to John Steinbeck's The Grapes of Wrath* acknowledge with thanks permission granted by the following publishers and journals to quote extensively from the books and articles named:

The Colorado Quarterly, for Bernard Bowron's *"The Grapes of Wrath*: A 'Wagons West' Romance," *from The Colorado Quarterly*, III (Summer, 1954), 84-91.

Holt, Rinehart and Winston, Inc., for Joseph Fontenrose's *John Steinbeck: An Introduction and Interpretation*, published by Barnes & Noble, Inc., 1963.

The Macmillan Company, for Joseph Warren Beach's *American Fiction 1920-1940*, published by The Macmillan Company, 1941.

University of Minnesota Press, for Charles Child Walcutt's *American Literary Naturalism, A Divided Stream*, published by the University of Minnesota Press, 1956.

Modern Fiction Studies, for Jules Chametzky's "The Ambivalent Endings of *The Grapes of Wrath*," from *Modern Fiction Studies*, XI (Spring, 1965), 34-44.

Oliver & Boyd Ltd., Edinburgh, Scotland, for F. W. Watt's *John Steinbeck*, Writers & Critics Series No. 16, published by Oliver & Boyd Ltd., 1962 (also published by Grove Press, Inc., 1962).

Rutgers University Press, for Peter Lisca's *The Wide World of John Steinbeck*, published by the Rutgers University Press, 1958.

Twayne Publishers, Inc., for Warren French's *John Steinbeck*, published by Twayne Publishers, Inc., 1961.

The Viking Press, for John Steinbeck, *The Grapes of Wrath*, published by The Viking Press, 1939.

CONTENTS

CHRONOLOGY

	Steinbeck	Other Writers	American History
1902	Born on February 27 in Salinas, California		
1919	Graduates from Salinas High School and works as a chemist in a sugar-beet plant		
1920	Enrolls at Stanford University (attends irregularly until 1925)	Eliot "Poems"; Fitzgerald, "This Side of Paradise"; Lewis, "Main Street"; Sandburg, "Smoke and Steel"	Senate fails to ratify League of Nations, waves of labor unrest, Sacco and Vanzetti affair, Prohibition begins (until 1933), U. S. population 106,000,000
1921	Is sporadically employed in California in a variety of jobs (until 1925)	Dos Passos, "Three Soldiers"; O'Neill, "Emperor Jones"	Warren G. Harding becomes President (1921-1923), 6,000,000 unemployed, Washington arms conference (1921-1922)
1922		Eliot, "Waste Land"; Lewis, "Babbitt"; O'Neill, "The Hairy Ape"	Formation of U.S.S.R.

	Steinbeck	Other Writers	American History
1923		Cather, "A Lost Lady"	Teapot Dome scandal, Calvin Coolidge becomes President (1923-1929), minimum wage law declared unconstitutional, agricultural overproduction
1924	Publishes two stories in the Stanford "Spectator"	Hemingway, "In Our Time"; Jeffers, "Tamar and Other Poems"	Hitler writes "Mein Kampf"
1925	Discontinues studies at Stanford, without a degree; works irregularly in New York City as a reporter and laborer	Cather, "The Professor's House"; Dos Passos, "Manhattan Transfer"; Dreiser, "An American Tragedy"; Fitzgerald, "The Great Gatsby"; Jeffers, "Roan Stallion"	Florida land boom; Scopes evolution trial in Dayton, Tennessee
1926	Returns to California to several different jobs, begins to write again	Faulkner, "Soldier's Pay"; Hemingway, "The Sun Also Rises"; Sandburg, "Abraham Lincoln, The Prairie Years"	
1927		Cather, "Death Comes for the Archbishop"; Hemingway, "Men Without Women"	Bill to improve farm prices vetoed, talking movies begin
1928		Benét, "John Brown's Body"; Frost, "West-Running Brook";	Kellogg-Briand peace pact, Muscle Shoals bill vetoed

Steinbeck	Other Writers	American History
	"The Hamlet of Archibald MacLeish"	
1929 "Cup of Gold: A Life of Henry Morgan, Buccaneer"	Faulkner, "The Sound and the Fury"; Hemingway, "A Farewell to Arms"; Wolfe, "Look Homeward, Angel"	Herbert Hoover becomes President (1929-1933), stock market crashes
1930 Marries Carrol Henning and lives in Pacific Grove, California; meets Ed Ricketts (marine biologist and model of several of Steinbeck's later fictional characters)	Crane, "The Bridge"; Dos Passos, "The 42nd Parallel"; Eliot, "Ash Wednesday"; "I'll Take My Stand" (by Southern agrarians)	Drought hurts already distressed farmers, U. S. population 123,000,000
1931	Buck, "The Good Earth"; Cather, "Shadows on the Rock"; Faulkner, "Sanctuary"	Worsening depression, tariffs reach new high, Al Capone imprisoned
1932 Moves to Los Angeles, "The Pastures of Heaven"	Caldwell, "Tobacco Road"; Dos Passos, "1919"; Farrell, "Young Lonigan"; MacLeish, "Conquistador"	Bonus army marches on Washington but is dispersed, Wisconsin first state to pass unemployment insurance law, Reconstruction Finance Corporation established
1933 Moves back to Pacific Grove, "To a God Unknown"	Hemingway, "Winner Take Nothing"; MacLeish, "Frescoes for Mr. Rockefeller's City"; Thurber, "My Life and Hard Times"	Franklin D. Roosevelt becomes President (1933-1945), "New Deal" begins, Prohibition repealed, emergency banking acts passed, U. S.

	Steinbeck	Other Writers	American History
			recognizes U.S.S.R., public power acts passed, Hitler takes over Germany
1934	Steinbeck's mother dies	Farrell, "Young Manhood of Studs Lonigan"	Farm acts passed, droughts cause dust bowl (1934-1937)
1935	"Tortilla Flat"	Anderson, "Winterset"; Farrell, "Judgment Day"; Glasgow, "Vein of Iron"; Lewis, "It Can't Happen Here"; MacLeish, "Panic"; Wolfe, "Of Time and the River"	WPA, Roosevelt locks horns with Supreme Court, CIO founded, Huey Long assassinated, Social Security Act
1936	Steinbeck's father dies, Steinbeck and his wife move to a Santa Cruz mountain ranch, "In Dubious Battle"	Dos Passos, "The Big Money"; Frost, "A Further Range"; Sandburg, "The People, Yes"	Soil Conservation Act, first sit-down strikes
1937	"Of Mice and Men," "The Red Pony" (parts published in magazine form in 1933); visits Ireland, Sweden, and Russia; successfully dramatizes "Of Mice and Men"; joins the Okies in their migration to California	MacLeish, "The Fall of the City"	Spanish Civil War, Japan invades China, Roosevelt tries to reorganize Supreme Court
1938	"The Long Valley," "Their Blood Is Strong"	Hemingway, "The Fifth Column and the First Forty-Nine Stories"; Sherwood,	Fair Labor Standards Act

	Steinbeck	Other Writers	American History
		"Abe Lincoln of Illinois"	
1939	"The Grapes of Wrath"	Sandburg, "Abraham Lincoln, The War Years"; Wolfe, "The Web and the Rock"	World War II begins
1940	Takes scientific voyage with Ricketts to Gulf of California	Brooks, "New England Indian Summer"; Clark, "Ox-Bow Incident"; Hemingway, "For Whom the Bell Tolls"; MacLeish, "The Irresponsibles"; Wolfe, "You Can't Go Home Again"; Wright, "Native Son"	Draft begins, U.S. exchanges destroyers for British bases, U.S. population 132,000,000
1941	"The Forgotten Village" (book version of film made in Mexico in 1940), "Sea of Cortez"	Fitzgerald, "Last Tycoon"; Hellman, "Watch on the Rhine"; Marquand, "H.M. Pulham, Esq."	Roosevelt "Four Freedoms" speech, Lend-Lease, Supreme Court upholds Fair Labor Standards Act of 1938, Atlantic Charter, Japanese attack Pearl Harbor, U.S. enters World War II (1941-1945)
1942	Divorced by Carol Steinbeck, "The Moon Is Down," "Bombs Away" (for U. S. Army Air Corps)	Faulkner, "Go Down, Moses"; Wilder, "Skin of Our Teeth"	Pacific coast Japanese relocated; major battles in Corregidor, Coral Sea, Midway, Solomons, Guadalcanal, North Africa; "Declaration by United Nations"
1943	Marries Gwyndolen Conger Verdon and	Dos Passos, "Number One"; Eliot,	Casablanca and Teheran conferences;

Steinbeck	Other Writers	American History
lives in New York City, becomes war correspondent for New York "Herald Tribune" in European Theater of Operations	"Four Quartets"; Pyle, "Here Is Your War"	major battles in North Africa, Sicily, Salerno
1944 Son Thomas born, "Lifeboat" (movie script)	Pyle, "Brave Men"; Shapiro, "V-Letter"	G.I. Bill; round-the-clock bombing of Germany; major battles in the Marshalls, northern Italy, the Marianas, Normandy, southern France, the Philippines; V-2 bombings of London
1945 "Cannery Row," "A Medal for Benny" (movie script), "The Red Pony" (republished in enlarged form)	Frost, "Masque of Reason"; Mauldin, "Up Front"; Williams, "Glass Menagerie"; Wright, "Black Boy"	Yalta conference; Harry S. Truman becomes President (1945-1953); major battles in Iwo Jima, Okinawa, France, Germany; Mussolini and Hitler die; V-E Day; Potsdam conference; Hiroshima and Nagasaki atom-bombed; V-J Day; Nuremberg war-crime trials (1945-1949)
1946 Son John born	Dreiser, "Bulwark"; Lowell, "Lord Weary's Castle"; Warren, "All the King's Men"	U.S. armed forces reduced, several major strikes, UNESCO founded
1947 Visits Russia with photographer	DeVoto, "Across the Wide Missouri";	Truman Doctrine, Marshall Plan,

Steinbeck	Other Writers	American History
Robert Capa, "The Wayward Bus," "The Pearl" (originally published in magazine form in 1945)	Frost, "Masque of Mercy"; Lewis, "Kingsblood Royal"; Williams, "Streetcar Named Desire"	Western Hemisphere Defense Treaty, Taft-Hartley Labor Relations Act
1948 Elected to the American Academy of Letters, divorced by Gwyndolen Steinbeck; Ricketts dies; "A Russian Journal" (with Capa)	Auden, "Age of Anxiety"; Cozzens, "Guard of Honor"; Faulkner, "Intruder in the Dust"; Mailer, "The Naked and the Dead"; Pound, "Pisan Cantos"	Massive foreign aid begins, Berlin blockade and airlift, House Committee on Un-American Activities, OAS formed
1949	Miller, "Death of a Salesman"	Russia explodes atom bomb, Point Four Plan, minimum wage raised to 75¢ an hour; NATO organized
1950 Marries Elaine Scott, "Burning Bright," "Viva Zapata!" (movie script)	Eliot, "Cocktail Party"	Korean War begins (1950-1953), U.S. population 151,000,000
1951 "The Log from the Sea of Cortez" (with tribute to Ricketts)	Faulkner, "Requiem for a Nun"; Jones, "From Here to Eternity"; Salinger, "Catcher in the Rye"; Styron, "Lie Down in Darkness"; Wouk, "Caine Mutiny"	22nd Amendment
1952 "East of Eden"	Ellison, "Invisible Man"; Hemingway, "The Old Man and	B-52 bomber developed, Supreme Court rules against

	Steinbeck	Other Writers	American History
		the Sea"; MacLeish, "Collected Poems"	subversives teaching in public schools; hydrogen bomb successfully tested by U.S.
1953		Bellow, "Augie March"; Eliot, "Confidential Clerk"	Dwight D. Eisenhower becomes President 1953-1961); Department of Health, Education, and Welfare established
1954	"Sweet Thursday"	Faulkner, "A Fable"; Stevens, "Collected Poems"; Welty, "Ponder Heart"	Supreme Court rules against "separate but equal" school facilities, SEATO organized, Senator J. R. McCarthy censured by U.S. Senate, Air Force Academy established
1955		Williams, "Cat on a Hot Tin Roof"	AFL and CIO merge, Salk anti-polio vaccine developed
1956		Kennedy, "Profiles in Courage"; O'Neill, "Long Day's Journey into Night"	Martin Luther King emerges as national leader of Negroes, Soil-Bank Act limits farm production
1957	"The Short Reign of Pippin IV"	Kerouac, "On the Road" Agee, "A Death in the Family"; Cozzens, "By Love Possessed"; Faulkner, "The Town";	Truman Doctrine extended to Middle East, labor racketeering investigated, Russia launches Sputnik, Little Rock race riots
1958	"'Once There Was a War" (World War II dispatches)	Eliot, "Elder Statesman"; MacLeish, "J.B."	U.S. orbits first satellite, U.S. intervenes in Lebanon

	Steinbeck	Other Writers	American History
1959			Alaska and Hawaii statehood, four-month steel strike, Castro becomes dictator of Cuba
1960	Takes a three-month trip by truck around U. S.	Faulkner, "The Mansion"; Michener, "Haawaii"; Styron, "Set This House on Fire"; Updike, "Rabbit, Run"	U.S. U-2 shot down by Russia, Vietnam Civil War begins, U.S. population 179,000,000
1961	"The Winter of Our Discontent"	Baldwin, "Nobody Knows My Name"; Salinger, "Franny and Zooey"	John F. Kennedy becomes President (1961-1963), 23rd Amendment, Peace Corps founded, Alliance for Progress proposed, Bay of Pigs disaster, first U.S. manned suborbital flight
1962	Receives the Nobel Prize for literature, "Travels with Charley"	Aibee, "Who's Afraid of Virginia Woolf"; Faulkner, "Reivers"; Porter, "Ship of Fools"; Williams, "Night of the Iguana"	First U.S. manned orbital flight, three-month New York newspaper strike, Supreme Court outlaws school prayers, Cuban crisis
1963	Has eye surgery	Updike, "The Centaur"	Nuclear Test-Ban Treaty, racial violence in Alabama, Kennedy assassinated, Lyndon B. Johnson becomes President (1963-)
1964	Receives U. S. Medal of Freedom	Bellow, "Herzog"; Hemingway, "Moveable Feast"	24th Amendment, Civil rights and antipoverty legislation,

	Steinbeck	Other Writers	American History
			Panama Canal Zone riots
1965		Mailer, "American Dream"	U.S. armed forces support South Vietnam, U.S. intervenes in Dominican Republic, riots in Watts section of Los Angeles, France jeopardizes NATO

Steinbeck's Life

THE MOST IMPORTANT THING to keep in mind about John Steinbeck is that at his best he is bleakly and yet bracingly honest. As a literary artist he has produced many works of varying merit. Some, like *Cup of Gold* and *Bombs Away,* now seem not likely to endure. Others, like *Tortilla Flat* and *Cannery Row,* are provocative but spotty. A few, like *Of Mice and Men, In Dubious Battle,* a few short stories, and —above all—*The Grapes of Wrath,* will probably enjoy literary immortality. But all of his works, good, bad, and indifferent, stem from personal experiences honestly thought through. Without a doubt, *The Grapes of Wrath* is his finest effort. It has the depressing savagery of naturalism at its most representative but with it the lift of a sober optimism.

Early Life

John Steinbeck was born in Salinas, California, on February 27, 1902. Salinas is a small farm town in the lush Salinas Valley east of Monterey Bay, and this general area has been the locale of most of the novelist's best work. His paternal grandfather, John Adolph Grossteinbeck, migrated from near Dusseldorf, Germany, to New Jersey and then

Florida, where his son John Erst Steinbeck was born. After service in the Confederate Army during the Civil War, Grossteinbeck went to Massachusetts and then in the 1870's established a flour mill in Hollister, California, a short distance northeast of Salinas.

Steinbeck's maternal grandfather, Samuel Hamilton, left his home near Londonderry, Ireland, and went around Cape Horn to California in the 1850's. A short time later his wife crossed the Isthmus of Panama and joined him. Their daughter Olive was born in San Jose. Before her marriage to John Steinbeck, Sr., Olive Hamilton was a schoolteacher at Big Sur and elsewhere in Monterey County. They married, had two daughters, then their only son—the future novelist— and finally a third daughter. If Steinbeck's mother was anything like the schoolteachers in his later fiction (those in *The Pastures of Heaven* and *To a God Unknown,* and Olive Hamilton in *East of Eden,* for example), she must have read good adventure fiction to her children. The father continued in the flour-milling business, and in the 1920's he also became the treasurer of Monterey County. He died in 1936, two years after his wife's death.

John Steinbeck grew up conditioned by a scene of magnificent natural beauty, making possible an abundance of outdoor activity, and also by the presence of good literature. The character of Jody, the juvenile hero of *The Red Pony,* is undoubtedly autobiographical in large part. Jody is not only sensitive but also tough, honest intellectually, and in tune with rugged nature about him. Steinbeck has always been the same, and those who see him either as so tough as to be divorced from subtle ideas or as occasionally so concerned with ideas as to become separated from reality, misunderstand him badly. Like Thoreau, he is keenly attuned to the worlds of contemplation and active nature both.

Steinbeck himself reports that his first important literary influences were the Bible, Malory's *Morte d'Arthur, Crime and Punishment, Madame Bovary, Paradise Lost,* and *The Return of the Native.* Later he began to like James Branch Cabell, Donn Byrne, D. H. Lawrence, Willa Cather, Sherwood Anderson, and Thackeray; still later, the Greek historians, Oriental sacred literature, Dante, and Goethe.

In 1919 Steinbeck graduated from the high school at Salinas, where he had been a track and basketball team member, contributor to the school paper, and president of the senior class. After a year's employment as an assistant in the chemical laboratory of a sugar-beet plant, which stimulated his lifelong interest in the biological sciences, he enrolled at Stanford University for parts of five years, gaining most from courses in classical literature, English, and zoology. In the intervals between terms of study, he worked as a ranch hand, road-gang laborer, sugar-mill hand, factory chemist, and the like. All of this varied experience was perfect preparation for a writer yet to be. In addition, it gave Steinbeck an indestructible faith in the common man.

Literary Apprenticeship

Quitting Stanford in 1925 without a degree, Steinbeck followed his already developed interest in writing—he had written some unsuccessful satirical stories and poems in college—and went to New York City, where he was a common laborer during the construction of Madison Square Garden, then an unsuccessful reporter and a free-lance writer before he soon beat a retreat back to his beloved California, where he became a caretaker of an estate at Lake Tahoe, then a fish-hatchery worker, and also an unemployed but tenacious writer of consistently rejected fiction.

After three discouraging years, Steinbeck was happy when Robert M. McBride & Co. of New York in August, 1929, published his swashbuckling quest romance called *Cup of Gold: A Life of Sir Henry Morgan, Buccaneer, with*

Occasional Reference to History. The stock market crash, which ended the Roaring Twenties a few months later, also spoiled the sales of Steinbeck's first novel. It was not until three years later that his second one appeared. It was *The Pastures of Heaven* (Brewer, Warren & Putnam, 1932), a strong episodic novel, cast authentically in California and telling about a cursed family and those who associate with it. By this time Steinbeck, married to Carol Henning since 1930, had known bitter poverty. He and his wife lived in Pacific Grove, on the coast due west of Salinas, in a house provided by his father, who also sent them $25 a month. Out of the depths of the Depression, Steinbeck produced *To a God Unknown* (Robert O. Ballou, 1933), which is a story with Biblical parallels and tells of literal self-sacrifice to make a waste land fertile again. Then Steinbeck wrote the first two parts of *The Red Pony* (first published in magazine form, 1933), about a boy who learns of life and death through his love for horses. Then came *Tortilla Flat* (Covici, Friede, 1935), a popular picaresque comedy about Danny and his semi-Arthurian gang of paisanos near Monterey. After the success of this intriguing work, Steinbeck never again knew poverty or critical neglect. Hollywood bought the film rights to it for $4,000, which was a great deal of money then.

In 1936, the childless Steinbecks moved from Pacific Grove to a ranch in the Santa Cruz mountains, visited Mexico for a brief time, and thus started what became a pattern of wandering for the novelist. Earlier in the same year his hard-hitting Salinas Valley strike novel, *In Dubious Battle,* was published by Covici, Friede. It caused a critical furor because, although it adversely portrays Communist agitators as selfishly placing party values above individual human rights, it also contains left-wing praise of strikers and denunciation of management.

Success

Then in 1937 *Of Mice and Men* (Covici, Friede) burst upon the reading public. Everyone knows about its hero George, a migrant farm hand, and his huge, moronic, pathetic companion Lennie, and how their dream of a little farm of their own is shattered because Lennie cannot resist caressing soft objects. Money from book clubs and Hollywood deluged Steinbeck and swept him into publicity which endangered his authorial anonymity. But the money also enabled him to go from California via the Panama Canal to New York and on to Ireland, Sweden, and Russia. Home again in the late summer, he finished a dramatization of his *Of Mice and Men* (with advice from George Kaufman), which won the Drama Critics' Circle prize for 1937. The following year Steinbeck's distinguished volume of short stories, called *The Long Valley,* was published by the Viking Press.

Next came *The Grapes of Wrath*. In the San Francisco *News* in October, 1936, Steinbeck had published a series of articles on the plight of migrant workers in the orchards and cotton fields near Salinas and in the Joaquin Valley (scene of Frank Norris's epic labor-strife novel *The Octopus*). A year later, shortly before *Of Mice and Men* hit the stage, Steinbeck drove to Oklahoma, joined the uprooted dust bowl victims from that state and from Arkansas in their trek west, lived in filthy Hoovervilles with them, and worked with them in California fields and orchards. The editors of *Occident* magazine asked for an article on the political aspects of the migrants' plight, but Steinbeck refused, saying that he did not want to generalize stupidly, that abstract terminology would be a mere escape, and that he was simply observing with intense sympathy a desperate human situation. Later he also decided against working with a *Life* magazine photographer on a series about the Okies, saying that he was absolutely unable to exploit their suffering for money. Then he decided to expand his San Francisco *News* essays, which he published as a pamphlet called "Their Blood Is Strong" early in 1938. Meanwhile he had been working on a satirical novel about migrants in California, to be called *L'affaire Lettuceberg,* which came to about 60,000 words by June, 1938. But Steinbeck was deeply dissatisfied with it. He recognized that he wanted epic sweep, not limited satire. He wanted his readers to see that his Okie friends were representative men and women, not objects to be hated.

So, like Melville mid-way through *Moby Dick,* Steinbeck refocused his chaotic material and turned it into a master-piece by the end of 1938. The new title, *The Grapes of Wrath,* struck him as exactly the right combination of soft and hard, of natural and militant. He suggested to his editor, Pascal Covici (by this time an executive of the Viking Press) that Julia Ward Howe's "Battle Hymn of the Republic," from which the title comes, be printed on the end papers.

The Grapes of Wrath was announced on the last day of 1938 in *Publishers' Weekly.* By the time it was published, on March 14, 1939, three pre-publication printings, totaling 50,000 copies, proved insufficient to meet the enormous demand. By May it was No. 1 on the best-seller list and was being bought at the phenomenal rate of 10,000 copies a week. By the end of the year it had sold more than 400,000 copies, and it placed eighth on the best-seller list in 1940. It has sold steadily in a variety of editions ever since.

Not everyone liked *The Grapes of Wrath.* Numerous official spokesmen for Oklahoma and California went to considerable pains to attack Steinbeck for inaccuracy. (At the same time, spokesmen for each state browbeat the other state for making possible the conditions which Steinbeck "inaccurately" pictured!) Political conservatives also attacked the novel as a piece of blatant Communist propaganda. And its frank and earthy diction was denounced by self-appointed censors as vile and obscene. So the sensational book was banned in certain quarters and was abundantly sold everywhere else.

Having done his part well, Steinbeck was rightly indifferent to criticism, adverse and favorable. Early in 1940 he went on a trip with Ed Ricketts, a biologist who was his best friend (he is the model for Dr. Burton of *In Dubious Battle* and for other figures in the fiction). The two went to the Gulf of California (also called the Sea of Cortez) to collect marine invertebrates. That summer Steinbeck went to Mexico City to help produce a movie called *The Forgotten Village,* his script for which (with pictures) was published in 1941, during which year Steinbeck also wrote and published *Sea of Cortez* (Viking) about his rollicking scientific tour. (Later, in 1951, Steinbeck published his *Log from the Sea of Cortez,* Viking, from which his part of *Sea of Cortez* was derived.)

Steinbeck next had an opportunity reluctantly to study another sort of animal which has long killed to survive— that is, man at war. World War II, which started in Europe in 1939, engulfed the United States two years later. Steinbeck was divorced by his first wife in 1942, and in the same year he published two war books. *Bombs Away: The Story of a Bomber Team* (Viking) is about the U.S. Army Air Force training program. (For film rights to it, Steinbeck received $250,000, all of which he generously made over to a trust fund for the Air Force Aid Society.) And *The Moon Is Down* (Viking) is his parable praising the powers of freedom against those of tyranny. Although Norway and Germany are not explicitly mentioned, it is obvious that the story was inspired by and concerns the Nazi occupation of Norway beginning in 1940. Steinbeck made the war-time mistake of endowing representatives of the enemy with human qualities. Still, Hollywood paid him $300,000 for the movie rights. A far better war allegory was the movie *Lifeboat* (released in 1944), for which Steinbeck provided the script. During half of 1943 Steinbeck was in Europe as a war correspondent. His New York *Herald Tribune* dispatches from England, Algiers, and Italy are graphic and sensible, having more of Ernie Pyle than of Tolstoy in them. (Ready the same year, Steinbeck's book of war reports did not appear until 1958, as *Once There Was a War,* published by Viking.) At about this time, Steinbeck visited President Franklin D. Roosevelt at the White House and suggested —but without success—flooding Nazi Germany with counterfeit German money as a means of disrupting that enemy country's economy.

In the spring of 1943 Steinbeck married Gwyndolyn Conger Verdon and for a long while thereafter made New York his home. His wife gave him two sons: Thomas, born in 1944, and John, born in 1946. Steinbeck bid farewell to California with *Cannery Row* (Viking, 1945), which has the same locale and epic idlers as *Tortilla Flat.* He once said that he wrote *Cannery Row* to distract the soldiers overseas from their boredom and fear. It does have an escapist quality, but (like *Tortilla Flat*) also grotesquely attacks the materialistic success drive and lustily praises raw fun.

Later Years

In 1947 Steinbeck published two quite different books. *The Wayward Bus* (Viking) is a morality novel filled with many negative but also several richly positive human types (including the Christ-like driver Juan Chicoy [note his initals]) careening through nature toward a modern Vanity Fair. And *The Pearl* (Viking) is a sentimental parable: a poor Indian named Kino finds a huge pearl which he thinks will be his salvation but which proves to be a curse, and at the end he is worse off than ever. Also in 1947 Steinbeck went with the famous *Life* magazine photographer Robert Capa to Russia, to observe and record their impressions. The result was *A Russian Journal,* published by Viking in 1948, the year of Steinbeck's second divorce.

Ever since *The Pearl,* Steinbeck has seemed to resemble its hero the pearl-diver, that is, to seek beneficent beauty only to find that it cannot satisfy him. Steinbeck wrote *Burning Bright* (Viking) in 1950; it is an unsatisfactory, even irresponsible thesis play-novelette, about which the less said the better. Late the same year Steinbeck married Elaine Scott. Two years later he published his biggest and most important novel since *The Grapes of Wrath.* It was *East of Eden* (Viking, 1952), which started as a fictionalized history of his maternal ancestors from the time of their arrival in California. Its original title was "Salinas Valley." Like Willa Cather with her *Sapphira and the Slave Girl,* Steinbeck late in his life seemed to be digging into old family memories. But then his book became a melodramatic, confused re-working of the Cain and Abel story. In 1954 Steinbeck published a weary, falsely positive sequel to *Cannery Row.* It is *Sweet Thursday* (Viking), as low and earthy as *Tortilla Flat, Of Mice and Men,* and *The Wayward Bus,* and therefore far removed from the mythic *East of Eden.* Like much of Faulkner's fiction, *Sweet Thursday* reworks characters previously introduced in earlier books. Next, in 1957, came Steinbeck's *Short Reign of Pippin IV* (Viking), a slightly silly fable of political power refused because it would cost the hero his integrity. Then came *The Winter of Our Discontent* (Viking, 1961), his latest big novel. It is an elaborate criticism of shoddy urban materialism, with so many parallels to religious, historical, and belletristic literature (note the title, from the opening line of Shakespeare's *Richard III*) that it is almost Joycean. And finally we have *Travels with Charley* (Viking,

1962), in which Steinbeck ramblingly reports his efforts to regain touch with his native land by means of a three-month trip late in 1960 by truck (named Rocinante after the steed of Cervantes's Don Quixote) accompanied only by a poodle.

In October, 1962, Steinbeck was awarded the Nobel Prize for literature. The prize committee mentioned among some of his other works *The Winter of Our Discontent* in its citation, but it was obvious to most critics and readers that Steinbeck had earned the high accolade by nothing so much as by *The Grapes of Wrath*.

John Steinbeck is still very much alive. It is dangerous to try to see a pattern in his works and then attempt to predict his future drift. But it is true that he has been alternating serious myth-redaction, in criticism of urban, materialistic America, with Rabelaisian nostalgia for an almost pastoral past. And it is also true that he uses his narrative power, which is sometimes clumsy (like Dreiser's) but always energetic (like Melville's), to help men and women of good will see themselves more honestly. In most of his works he may be imagined as saying with Emerson, "We grant that human life is mean, but how did we find out that it was mean?" ("The Over-Soul"). Steinbeck, like the best naturalists, shows us the meanness so that we will work toward something more ideal, more in keeping with the American dream. Perhaps we may hope that he will give us more good fiction based on biology and legends, and full of grime, hard knuckles, and a warm sense of brotherhood. It will have to be very good indeed to be worthy of standing beside his masterpiece, *The Grapes of Wrath*.

THE GRAPES OF WRATH:

Its Importance

The Grapes of Wrath is important as a proletarian novel, as a naturalistic document, and as enduring art.

Proletarian literature, as John D. Hart says, comes from a school of writing which "contends that experience is primarily conditioned by the social, economic and political environment and that the author is able to understand this environment by Marxist theory, which explains the dialectical relation of class cultures to the prevailing economic and social structure. During the Depression, when they flourished, proletarian writers contended that it is life itself, not the Communist party, that forced them to be interested in such phenomena as strikes, agricultural and industrial conditions, and persecution and oppression of racial minorities and the working class." [1]

How does all of this apply to Steinbeck's novel? Steinbeck takes one social unit, the Joad family, and shows how it is forced to move west by adverse economic conditions in eastern Oklahoma. The Joads are social outcasts both on

---

[1]James D. Hart, *The Oxford Companion to American Literature,* 4th ed. (New York: Oxford University Press, 1965), p. 680.

11

the way west and in California once they arrive. They have no choice but to associate with "have-not's" who are similar to themselves, and they are totally incapable of establishing any social relationships with the propertied and managerial classes there. Inevitably, therefore, the Joads begin to see the necessity of banding together with their kind in a social and economic struggle against the "have's." In this effort toward union, they are oppressed by those in political power and by their deputies. Steinbeck is not concerned here (as he was in his earlier novel *In Dubious Battle*) with showing the success of Communist agitation and organization. He ridicules the property owners who shout "red" at every migrant who wants a decent wage, and he has Tom Joad laughingly call himself a red for wanting such a wage himself. Obviously neither Tom nor Jim Casy knows the first thing about Marx and Communism. Steinbeck's concern here, like that of the Joads and Casy, is with life rather than politics. And by use of the interchapters (also called intercalary chapters) Steinbeck expands his view to include not merely the Joads but thousands of other migrants like them. The interchapters show that property in California was acquired by force in the first place and that property rights both there and in Oklahoma have been wrongly made to seem more important than human rights. His point is obviously the Emersonian one that in a world where there is "Law for man, and law for thing," human rights should take precedence over property rights. Otherwise, as Emerson goes on to say in his "Channing Ode," "Things are in the saddle,/And ride mankind."

Naturalistic novels, as a distinguished literary handbook points out, "have tended to emphasize either a biological determinism, with an emphasis on the animal nature of man, particularly his heredity, portraying him as an animal engaged in the endless and brutal struggle for survival, or a socio-economic determinism, portraying man as the victim of environmental forces and the product of social and economic factors beyond his control or his full understanding." [2]

Surely *The Grapes of Wrath* qualifies as naturalistic. Its most effective symbol is probably the land turtle which heads southwest and plods along unceasingly. This turtle represents the Joads specifically, and the unstoppable people in general. Over and over, animal imagery is used to suggest the essentially animal quality of man and, more specifically, the bestial level to which the Joads have been reduced by socio-economic forces. The Joads are certainly victims of their environment, both natural and man-made. The drought and resulting dust have ruined their crops. When they cannot continue to pay their mortgages, the bank must dispossess them. And the tractors must push over their house and drive them off the land, so that, for a profit, all little farms may be combined and worked more efficiently by modern methods. Thus little people are at the mercy of the monsters—the bank and the tractor. Steinbeck says that men made the bank but cannot control it, and further, that the tractor is a relentless beast which depersonalizes its driver into a mere robot. On the road to California, the Joads are partly dehumanized by a whole array of adverse forces which are both man-made and natural. They are at the mercy of yet another machine, their ancient Hudson car turned truck, which they must pamper like an unpredictable god. They are cheated at almost every turn. Nature is often pitiless. They must drive across torrid deserts and over jagged mountains which seem malevolent. When they get to California and lush valleys seem to hold out the promise of milk and honey at last, it is the some old story: those who have property are afraid that those who have not will demand by force what they need for survival. Neither side has imagina-

---

[2]William Flint Thrall, Addison Hibbard, and C. Hugh Holman, *A Handbook to Literature* (New York: Odyssey, 1936, 1960), p. 303.

tion or objectivity sufficient to permit any kind of understanding.

If *The Grapes of Wrath* were simply a naturalistic, proletarian novel, it would long ago have faded from the scene. Responsible for its continuing popularity is its artistry. In this novel, Steinbeck has created memorable characters, especially Ma Joad, her son Tom, and the idealistic ex-preacher Jim Casy. In addition, minor figures like Grampa, Muley Graves, the unnamed used-car salesman, and the truckers' waitress Mae are set vividly before us. Steinbeck characterizes by description, dialogue, and action. He regularly sketches the physical appearance of a given character, lets him painfully articulate his half-formed thoughts in accurately reported speech, and puts him through his part in the plot. Since Steinbeck is dealing with impoverished and almost illiterate characters from the lowest segments of society, their appearance, talk, and conduct are crude by standards "higher" than their own. But their hopes and fears are elemental and therefore resemble those of most of us far more than we might like to admit. Farfetched though it may seem, it is true that Steinbeck's major characters here have a kind of stark, Biblical dignity. And their epic trek across half a continent is thrilling, like all great journey literature. Steinbeck gives us scenery to match the awesome dimensions of the trip: the dust bowl, rolling plains, the desert, life-giving rivers, high mountains, and then valleys of incredible beauty and fertility. Finally, like all great art, *The Grapes of Wrath* has a message of transcendent importance. What that message is, each reader ought to decide largely for himself. Is it a Darwinian one, that life is a teeming jungle in which only the hardiest survive? Is it a political one about the obligation of the fortunate to share the fruits of the good earth? Is it simply an ethical one to the effect that the Joads are a human unit imperiled and partly defeated but inevitably growing toward a realization that they are an integral part of the great family of man?

The Grapes of Wrath is memorable for telling the story of the Joad family. The intercalary chapters require us to see that the Joads are typical of other unfortunate people hurt by a specific national disaster. In turn, the entire Okie misery of the late 1930's is a tragedy which is representative of the plight of mankind whenever nature seems to abandon it. The moral is obvious. Mankind must not abandon itself but must use all its ingenuity to ameliorate its position.

THE GRAPES OF WRATH:

Chapter-by-Chapter Summary
and Critical Commentary

Chapter 1   Summary

It is spring in Oklahoma. The gentle rains lift the corn. But by the end of May the clouds disappear and the sun begins to flare down and parch the land. In June the corn turns brown and withers. Dust fluffs up, and the wind begins to carry the soil away. Dust is everywhere, and the mid-day sun is red.

Men and women have to protect their noses with handkerchiefs and their eyes with goggles. The dust sifts into their houses. When the children go outside, they do not run and shout. Instead, they stand beside their parents and move their bare feet through the dust. The men go to their fences and survey the ruined corn. The women follow but look only at the men's faces. Will the men break this time? When their faces look puzzled but also angry and resistant, the women know that the men will not break yet.

Commentary

This short chapter introduces the reader to the cause of the migration of the Joad family (as yet unnamed) to California. Adverse weather conditions are turning Oklahoma farms into a waste land. Implicit already is the suggestion that if nature turns against man, the people must band together and help each other. Verbs like *flare, struck,* and *dug* (having to do with the sun and the wind) suggest the ferocity of nature, which seems to be man's adversary.

From the Critics

"The dust which is mentioned twenty-seven times in three pages of Chapter 1 comes to stand not only for the land itself, but also for the basic situation out of which the novel's action develops." [1]

"As the book opens, a description of drought immediately sets the tone of sterility; Chapter One is peppered with references to the sun, ants, weeds, dust, and wind, and the colors red and grey predominate. Dead corn lies scattered about. Rain in sufficient quantity has not fallen on mother earth. On the cosmic level, then, there is no reproduction." [2]

Chapter 2   Summary

A heavy-set truck driver jokes with the waitress in a restaurant, then bangs the screen door shut, and approaches his huge red truck. A young man with cheap new clothes is waiting and asks him for a lift, in spite of a *No Riders* sign on the truck. He explains that "sometimes a guy'll be

---

[1]Peter Lisca, *The Wide World of John Steinbeck* (New Brunswick, New Jersey: Rutgers University Press, 1958), p. 158. Reprinted with permission.

[2]Theodore Pollock, "On the Ending of 'The Grapes of Wrath,'" *Modern Fiction Studies,* IV (Summer, 1958), 177.

a good guy even if some rich bastard makes him carry a sticker." The driver lets him in and soon is inquisitively but harmlessly asking questions. He is surprised to learn that the hitch-hiker's father is a forty-acre sharecropper who has not yet been dusted out or tractored out. The hitch-hiker says that he has been away for four years. When the driver notices his shiny hands and says that he must have been swinging a pick or a sledge, the man gets annoyed and sarcastically introduces himself as Tom Joad. The driver retreats behind the excuse that his job is lonely and hard. Soon he is aimlessly chatting again, about a friend who loved big words, then about his own powers of observation; and then he adds that he would like to study and become a fingerprint expert. This arouses the animosity of Tom, who says that the driver is as nosy as a sheep in a vegetable patch. As he gets out at a dirt crossroad leading to his farm home, Tom quickly adds that he has been serving time at McAlester, the Oklahoma state prison, for homicide. "I'm sprung in four for keepin' my nose clean."

Commentary

This chapter introduces edgy Tom Joad, one of the three main characters in the novel. It also foreshadows the fate, soon to be revealed, of the Joad forty-acre farm: what the dust has not already killed, the tractors will soon finish off. Further, this chapter suggests that the have-not's, like Tom and the truck driver, ought to stick together against the rich.

From the Critics

". . . Tom as a person has two distinct personalities, a public and a private one, the public one a cruel toughness that he displays to strangers (like the truckdriver who gives him his first ride, and the one-eyed junkyard attendant he insults [Chapter 16]) and the private one a surprising tenderness he displays to his family." [3]

Chapter 3   Summary

Out of the tangled dry grass along the edge of the concrete highway comes a horny land turtle with "fierce, humorous eyes." He slowly claws his way up the embankment and onto the pavement. When a red ant runs into his shell, he quickly crushes it. (Ma later crushes an ant bothering Granma [Chapter 18].) A head of wild oats clings between the shell and a front leg. The turtle plods across the scorching concrete. A women driver swerves to avoid it, and dust boils up behind her sedan. Then a light truck approaches. Its driver deliberately aims at the turtle, which spins onto his back when a front wheel hits the edge of his shell. (When driving later, Al aims at but misses a cat and Tom has to hit a rabbit [Chapter 16]. At other times also, they aim at objects in the road.) But the turtle wiggles back to his feet again, crawls on, drops some spearheaded oat seeds by chance, and rakes dirt over them as he moves on.

Commentary

This significant little chapter is important for several reasons. First of all, Steinbeck scientifically describes the turtle and other forms of life with an accuracy which enhances our faith in him as a realistic writer in general. Next, implicit in this passage is Steinbeck's naturalistic philosophy: the turtle is determined to persevere, and in the process he dispassionately crushes opposing ants and sows seeds of

---

[3]Stanley Edgar Hyman, "Some Notes on John Steinbeck," *The Antioch Review*, II (Summer, 1942), 195-196.

future oat life. Also, the migration of the turtle prefigures the migration of the Okies in general and the Joads in particular (see Chapter 6). Finally, the seemingly gratuitous details of the truck driver and the woman driver may intentionally suggest Steinbeck's awareness that men are often destructive while women are usually more protective: Tom Joad has just been revealed as having committed manslaughter; later we shall see that Ma Joad and Rose of Sharon try to preserve the family and nurture life.

From the Critics

"Very early in the book the author devotes a whole chapter — a short one — to the picture of a turtle crossing the highway. It is an act of heroic obstinacy and persistence against heavy odds. This is a gem of minute description, of natural history close-up, such as would delight the reader of Thoreau or John Burroughs." [4]

"In *The Grapes of Wrath* there is the parable of the tortoise crossing the highway. Knocked by a car, carried off by Tom Joad, beaten by sun and wind, he is the People; he struggles on indomitably, and he probably in the end reaches his destination." [5]

"This turtle is also [like the people] indestructible. . . . The turtle is of course the Life Force itself: tireless, indestructible, dispersing everywhere the seeds of life. But by a series of contrived associations, Steinbeck makes clear that the turtle is also the Joads — or that they are it . . ." [6]

---

[4]Joseph Warren Beach, *American Fiction 1920-1940* (New York: Macmillan, 1941), p. 333.

[5]Charles Child Walcutt, *American Literary Naturalism, A Divided Stream* (Minneapolis: University of Minnesota Press, 1956), p. 268. Reprinted with permission.

[6]Bernard Bowron, *"The Grapes of Wrath:* A 'Wagons West' Romance," *The Colorado Quarterly,* III (Summer, 1954), 85. Reprinted with permission.

Chapter 4 Summary

Tom hears the truck move off, then has a drink of whisky from his pint bottle, takes off his tight new shoes and bundles them in his coat, and walks on through the dust. He sees a land turtle and wraps him in the coat. To get out of the hammering rays of the sun, he aims for a tattered willow tree but finds Jim Casy, the preacher who baptized him, stretched in the shade there, singing "Yes, sir, that's my Saviour," to the tune of "Yes, Sir, That's My Baby." Casy has a neck as stringy as a celery stalk, a very high forehead, and eloquent hands.

After the two men recognize each other, Tom sits beside Casy and offers him a drink. Soon the two are reminiscing. Casy explains that he quit being a preacher, because every time he would get a congregation together, jumping, talking in tongues, and glory-shouting, he would take a girl all full of grace into the grass and lie with her there. Tom says laconically that perhaps he should have been a preacher. But Casy goes on seriously and voices his slowly evolved belief that there is no sin and no virtue. "There's just stuff people do. It's all part of the same thing. And some of the things folks do is nice, and some ain't nice, but that' as far as any man got a right to say." He does not know anyone named Jesus, he adds, but only a number of stories about Him. Casy says that he loves the people. "Maybe all men got one big soul ever' body's a part of." Tom drops his eyes before such naked honesty.

Then Tom begins to discuss himself. Casy is not inquisitive, but he is sympathetic when Tom explains that he killed a man. Both were drunk, and when the other fellow stabbed him, he smashed his head with a nearby shovel. Casy wonders if he is ashamed of having done so. Tom replies that he is not. When Casy wonders about prison life, Tom explains that the food was regular, the clothes were clean, baths were available, but there were no women. He adds that one man when released missed the security of jail life so much that he deliberately stole a car to be caught and returned to prison.

Tom starts to continue walking to his home. Casy decides to join him, since he wants to see Tom's father again. They walk together pleasantly through the golden light of late afternoon. Tom drones on about how his father stole their house. It was an abandoned wooden structure which he sawed in half and dragged with twelve horses and two mules to his forty acres, now all fenced with wire. Then Tom tells about his wild-uncle, Uncle John, who traded Tom's father the spools of wire for a young pig, which he butchered at once, began to cook, and tried to eat entirely, only to get sick. Tom's father salted down what was left. Suddenly Tom sees the Joad place beyond a hill. It looks different. No one is there.

Commentary

This chapter is important mainly for introducing the ex-preacher Jim Casy, another of the three main characters of the novel. He is an unwashed Emersonian, and his initials are probably meant to suggest his Christ-like qualities, which will become apparent toward the close of the story (see especially Chapter 26). In addition, this chapter serves to advance the plot. Tom is getting closer to home, or what is left of it. The animal imagery in this chapter should be noted: Casy has "great horse teeth"; a person with religion is sometimes as "Jumpy as a stud horse in a box stall"; at one point "Pa lets out a squawk like a sow litterin' broken bottles"; etc.

From the Critics

"Mr. Steinbeck almost always in his fiction is dealing either with the lower animals or with human beings so rudimentary that they are almost on the animal level." [7]

"From the opening passages . . . to the last scene in which an attempt is made to beatify Rose of Sharon's biological act, the narrative is richly interspersed with literal and figurative zoology." [8]

"Casy resembles Emerson more than he does Sinclair Lewis' Elmer Gantry or Erskine Caldwell's Semon Dye. For like Emerson, Casy discovers the Oversoul through intuition and rejects his congregation in order to preach to the world." [9]

". . . Casy, the Okie preacher, utters thoroughly transcendental statements of the perfection and universality of spirit, and Tom Joad toward the end of the story speaks the same language . . ." [10]

"Casy has given up the negative or legalistic aspects of Christianity to endorse its spirit; the metaphysics of Christianity he exchanges for those of Emersonian transcendentalism. . . . In his turn Tom Joad hears this 'call' too." [11]

"With the story of the Joads is intertwined that of the Holinist preacher Jim Casy, whose experience, meant apparently as a parallel to that of Jesus of Nazareth, is actually less a parallel than a shocking travesty." [12]

---

[7]Edmund Wilson, *The Boys in the Back Room: Notes on California Novelists* (San Francisco: Colt Press, 1941), pp. 42-43.

[8]George Bluestone, *Novels into Film* (Baltimore: Johns Hopkins Press, 1957), p. 150.

[9]Lisca, *Wide World of Steinbeck*, p. 175.

[10]Walcutt, *American Literary Naturalism*, p. 263.

[11]F. W. Watt, *John Steinbeck* (New York: Grove, 1962), p. 71. Reprinted with permission.

[12]Walter Fuller Taylor, *The Story of American Letters*, rev. ed. (Chicago: Regnery, 1956), p. 459.

". . . Casy represents a contemporary adaptation of the Christ image, and . . . the meaning of the book is revealed through a sequence of Christian symbols." [13]

Chapter 5   Summary

This is a general chapter, with no characters named. It describes the legal situation in Oklahoma during the dust storms and drought. Soft-fingered landowners in closed cars are pitted against hard-handed, impoverished tenant farmers. And both are forced to do the bidding of the man-made monster, the bank, which no man can seem to control. "The bank is something else than men. It happens that every man in a bank hates what the bank does, and yet the bank does it. The bank is something more than men . . . It's the monster. Men made it, but they can't control it."

From the East comes an order to the bankers to make the land produce a profit (the food of the bank). The bank hires a man to drive a remorseless tractor straight through the farms and farm houses. The man follows his orders, for three dollars a day, because he has a wife and children to feed. The perplexed tenant farmers argue that their grandfathers fought Indians here, that their fathers were born here, that they fought snakes and weeds and adverse weather, and that this is their home. They threaten to shoot the tractor driver. He merely says that their houses would still be bumped down, and they would be hanged for murder, that the bank president himself takes orders from the East. "But where does it stop? Who can we shoot?" the bewildered farmers ask.

They begin to understand the matter. When a man owns something which he can walk on and handle and be sad about

---

[13]Martin Shockley, "Christian Symbolism in *The Grapes of Wrath*," *College English*, XVIII (November, 1956), 87.

when it is not doing well, then it is a part of him. But when a man has property which he cannot get his fingers in or walk on, then it owns him. However, the farmers do not yet know what they can do about this misery. One of them says, "We all got to figure. There's some way to stop this. It's not like lightning or earthquakes. We got a bad thing made by men, and by God that's something we can change."

Nevertheless, the tractor grinds on and one farm home after another is crushed, and the victims only stand by and stare.

Commentary

This is a highly naturalistic chapter, with the enemy of the people taking on the contours of a Frankenstein's monster, as with Zola's mine, Crane's war machine, and Norris's railroad and wheat-pit. Steinbeck's dialogue here is noteworthy for its abstract, expressionistic quality, like that in O'Neill's *Hairy Ape,* for example. And as other optimistic naturalistic writers do, Steinbeck suggests that "There's some way to stop" the enemies of mankind, if people will only get together "to figure."

From the Critics

"In *The Grapes of Wrath* he [Steinbeck] has a tenant farmer say something in which it is not preposterous to find a faint echo of Leo XIII's teaching on property in his encyclical letter *On the Condition of the Working Classes:* 'If a man owns a little property, that property is him, it's part of him, and it's like him. . . . ' Is it fantastic to see some similarity between this and the words of Pope Leo: 'When man spends the industry of his mind and the strength of his body in procuring the fruits of nature, by that act he makes his own that portion of nature's field which he cultivates . . .'?" [14]

"Chapter 5 is mostly a dialogue between two generalized forces, the banks and the farmers, presenting in archetype the conflict in which the Joads are caught up." [15]

"The Oklahoma land company is . . . one of the monsters of Chapter Five . . . The monster is the sort of organism that absorbs its members, drains them of their individualities, and makes them into organization men. The tractor is the monster visible . . ." [16]

Chapter 6   Summary

Tom and Casy walk into the battered Joad house at sundown. All is ruined and deserted. The well is dry, and the barn is filled with mice. In the empty house, Tom picks up reminders of the family past, for example, one of his mother's shoes. He releases his turtle, and it immediately plods off southwest. Then an old friend, Muley Graves, walks cautiously out of the cotton field, and Tom greets him.

Soon Muley explains that all the Joads, driven from their land by a tractor, are at their Uncle John's place, eight miles away, and are chopping cotton for money to buy a car to go to California in. Tom's father was worried and thought of writing Tom in prison about their plans; but instead he asked Muley to watch out for Tom and tell him. Muley is determined never to leave his land.

---

[14]John S. Kennedy, "John Steinbeck: Life Affirmed and Dissolved," in *Fifty Years of the American Novel: A Christian Appraisal,* ed. by Harold C. Gardiner, S. J. (New York: Scribner's, 1952), pp. 222-223.

[15]Lisca, *Wide World of Steinbeck,* p. 156.

[16]Joseph Fontenrose, *John Steinbeck: An Introduction and Interpretation* (New York: Barnes & Noble, 1963), p. 71. Reprinted with permission.

When Tom says that he is hungry, Muley shares his sack of three rabbits, which Tom expertly skins and begins to cook, throwing the entrails to a shadowy gray cat nearby. Muley voices his absolute inability to leave the land where his father died. Casy philosophizes, out of preacher habit, and seems to be coming close to a momentous truth about all the helpless farm families bereft of their homes. At Tom's bidding, they fall ravenously on their crisp meal. Tom tells Muley that if he had to kill again in self-protection, he would do so; he adds that a prison term taught him nothing.

Suddenly headlights are seen bobbing up into the dark sky. Muley urges the other two to run into the cotton field. Little though Tom likes to hide in a patch his family once tilled, he does so with Muley and Casy, since he is on parole and cannot afford a fight with the authorities. The car draws up, with a spotlight. Muley enjoys outwitting the deputies, who soon drive away. Then Muley leads them to a safe cave, which Tom remembers digging with his brother Noah. Muley hides in it, to be safe. Tom refuses to be cooped up and lies down outside. Casy sits, stares at the stars, and ponders. As silence falls, the wild night creatures begin to scamper and flutter.

Commentary

The previous chapter told in general terms what happens to farm families when the banks drive them off their land. Chapter 6 brings the misery down to the personal level of one such family, the Joads. But since Muley tells Tom about past events, it may be said that the action of the novel proper has not yet really begun. Chapter 6 contains a good deal of gratuitous information of a general nature: how the hot, clear sky darkens at twilight, how Tom skins rabbits, how a wooden shack cracks in the cool night air. Part of Steinbeck's purpose in this novel is to be informative concerning an area and a way of life not universally known. Tom's refusal to hide in the cave gains point when we read in Chapter 28 that Tom is obliged to hide in such a cave near a culvert in California, to escape detection by the authorities.

From the Critics

"The migrants were leaving the graves of their ancestors behind them, personified in Muley Graves. He was stubborn, as his nickname indicates, and he refused to leave the country, although he had no house to live in." [17]

"An extreme example of the [Russian] critics' enthusiasm [for *The Grapes of Wrath*] was Miller-Budnitskaya's comparison of the weird and demented character, Muley Graves, to Robin Hood: 'Like this legendary hero of the Anglo-Saxon yeoman, banished from the land by the Norman barons, Muley is a rebel. In token of social protest he goes off into the forest and declares partisan war on the sheriff and the law.' " [18]

Chapter 7   Summary

Here the scene is a used-car lot. The high-pressure owner orders his assistants to roll up their sleeves and pitch in, soften up potential customers—usually evicted tenant farmers anxious to purchase cheap jalopies to drive to California—and send them on to him, rush the mere gawkers and critics off the lot, hide tire bruises, and put sawdust into

---

[17]Fontenrose, *Steinbeck,* pp. 81-82.

[18]Deming Brown, *Soviet Attitudes Toward American Writing* (Princeton, New Jersey: Princeton University Press, 1962), p. 79.

transmissions and gears to muffle their racket. The place is a graveyard of automotive junk, with pigweed growing through broken engine blocks and with bent exhaust pipes lying about like snakes. The farmers pay up to eighty dollars for worthless wrecks, often sign high-rate notes, get nowhere with complaints later, and drive the battered evidence out of the state. The salesman's mottoes are "If I had enough jalopies I'd retire in six months" and "We sell 'em, but we don't push 'em home."

Commentary

This vicious little chapter shows man set against man for a profit and hints at the difficulty the Joads must face when they buy a car to take them west.

Chapter 8   Summary

Now Tom and Casy are walking in the pre-dawn light toward Uncle John's place, where Muley Graves said the Joads are temporarily staying. Tom is excited to be near his family again. He tells Casy how Uncle John was once married. When his pregnant wife complained of stomach pains and asked for a doctor, Uncle John dosed her with pain killer and she died of a ruptured appendix. The bitter memory has made Uncle John queer, and he now goes about doing unusually kind things, for example, giving gum to children. He also goes on wild drinking and woman-chasing sprees once in a while.

The two men next see some sexually excited dogs, including the tough Joad dog Flash. Then they talk about bulls and heifers, and Casy says he is happy that he is no longer a preacher, since people now talk frankly to him and he can even cuss when he wants to.

The sun comes up and lights Casy's face and then reveals a Hudson Super-Six car (converted into a truck) in Uncle John's hard dirt yard. Tom creeps up on his father (called Old Tom and Pa), who is working on the car. He is grizzled, black-eyed, lean, powerful, and intent. He slowly but then joyously recognizes his son, asks at once if he has broken out of prison and is therefore in hiding, and then excitedly suggests that they surprise Ma. He politely welcomes Casy. Then Pa and Tom walk to the noisy kitchen and ask Ma if two strangers can have breakfast. She invites them in without looking up from her sizzling pork, high biscuits, and tumbling coffee.

Ma is heavy from child-bearing, but not fat. Her thin gray hair is gathered in a knot in back. Her hands are chubby, delicate, girlish. Her loose Mother Hubbard is long and gray, and shapeless. She is barefooted. She is "the citadel of the family." As long as she is firm, the family is secure. When she dances, the others are happy. She has a calm beyond joy or pain.

When Ma finally looks up and sees Tom, her eyes widen, her mouth flies open, and she breathes out, "Thank God." She quickly asks whether he is legally free, then feels his arm muscles, then fingers his cheek as a blind person might, and then turns back to her cooking for a moment. This gives Pa a chance to explain to Tom that Grampa and Granma are sleeping in the barn now, to avoid disturbing the children when they have to get up in the night. Pa runs off to give them the good news of Tom's return. Ma now asks Tom shyly whether jail has rotted him, has made him "mean-mad." Tom says that he is all right, that he is not proud, that he holds no grudges. Ma is immensely relieved. She says that she knew Purty Boy Floyd (occasionally mentioned later), who was only normally wild as a youngster until the authorities caught him doing "a little bad thing" and hurt him so much that he turned into a mad coyote and had to be run down and killed.

As Granma is heard bleating out "Pu'raise Gawd fur vittory!", Tom notes a change in his mother. She is bitterly resentful that the authorities have run her family out of their own house. She says that a hundred thousand tenants have been similarly evicted. Then she dimly expresses the notion that they should all have united: "If we was all mad the same way, Tommy—they wouldn't hunt nobody down . . . "

Spry old Grampa comes rushing up, buttoning his fly wrong and winking his bad-boy, mischievous, lecherous little eyes. Granma scurries after him, noisily and affectionately. Noah, Tom's older brother, comes up gently. Noah is tall, very quiet, strange, and slightly twisted, ever since the day Pa assisted at his painful birth and pulled his head out of shape.

As the meal is about to start, the Joads call Casy, who has kept himself considerately at a distance, but who wants to join the family and go west with it. Granma shrilly demands that he say grace, and then bleats "A-men" and "Hallelujah" when he pauses during his philosophical, non-religious little speech of gratitude. Casy says that he is as confused as Jesus was in the wilderness. He concludes as follows: "I got thinkin' how we was holy when we was one thing, an' mankin' was holy when it was one thing."

Then they all crunch and slurp their food. Then the men go out to the truck. Pa explains that Al, Tom's younger, mechanically inclined brother, has tinkered with the motor and says it is reliable. Al is now off "Tom-cattin' hisself to death," Pa adds. Grampa lecherously praises Al and says that he was worse when he was Al's age. Then Tom learns that Ruthie and Winfield, the youngest Joad children, are in town (Sallisaw, Oklahoma) selling equipment with Uncle John. Another sister, Rose of Sharon (always called Rosasharn), is staying with the Rivers family, since she is now married to Connie Rivers and is expecting a baby—in three or four or five months, Pa explains vaguely. The men discuss their plans to start their trek west soon.

Al struts up cockily, until he recognizes his heroic brother Tom, whom he holds in awe for having killed a man. Then Al drops the swagger and imitates Tom's prison-face stoicism. They shake hands. Al seems disappointed when he learns that Tom did not bust out of jail but was merely paroled.

Commentary

This chapter is important for plot and characterization. Tom's reunion with his parents is intensely moving, especially with Ma. (Ma Joad is, with her son Tom and Casy, one of the three main characters of the novel.) Ma is so grateful when she sees his safe return that Tom, quietly emotional himself, bites his lip until it bleeds. Ma's feeling his face as a blind person might is a foreshadowing of her later farewell to Tom in the dark of the California culvert cave (Chapter 28). In addition, Grampa, Granma, Pa, Noah, and Al are all skillfully introduced and sketched in Chapter 8. Their dialect is excellently recorded. The bucolic gaiety of Grampa is notable. He wants to go to California and squash grapes all over his face. This is the first of many references to grapes in the novel.

From the Critics

"Pa was the representative of practical prudence; Ma the voice of right feeling and generous impulse and the traditional code of decent conduct."[19]

---

[19]Beach, *American Fiction*, p. 346.

"In Ma Joad, Steinbeck created one of the most memorable characters in American fiction of the twentieth century. It is her courage which sustains the family through the almost overwhelming distresses suffered during their epic migration to the West. She voices the author's belief in the common folk's invincible will to survive . . ." [20]

"As an extreme case of the isolated individual against the world the story of Pretty Boy Floyd is mentioned again and again [in *The Grapes of Wrath*]. . . . But the Okies of this novel do not turn into that sort of outlaw. Driven out of the home and the society they once knew, wandering in isolation among those who cannot even accept them as members of a common humanity, they can only turn to each other for help and understanding and love." [21]

"This Biblical structure [Egypt, Exodus, Canaan] is supported by a continuum of symbols and symbolic actions. The most pervasive symbolism is that of grapes. The novel's title, taken from 'The Battle Hymn of the Republic,' . . . is itself a reference to Revelation [14:19] . . ." [22]

Chapter 9   Summary

Here is pictured a general family selling its agricultural tools, animals, and household possessions, all at a dreadful loss. "Well, take it — all junk — and give me five dollars. You're not buying only junk, you're buying junked lives." The ruined tenants realize that they cannot start all over

---

[20]Lyon N. Richardson, George H. Orians, and Herbert R. Brown, eds., *The Heritage of American Literature,* 2 vols. (Boston: Ginn, 1951), II, 818.

[21]Edwin T. Bowden, *The Dungeon of the Heart: Human Isolation and the American Novel* (New York: Macmillan, 1961), p. 147.

[22]Lisca, *Wide World of Steinbeck,* p. 169.

again elsewhere, stripped of everything that went to create a home. "How can we live without our lives?" But into a trailer they pile the few possessions they must take along (including the family rifle), burn everything else, and bitterly drive away. "And some day—the armies of bitterness will all be going the same way."

Commentary

This intercalary chapter is like the previous odd-numbered ones, all of which prefigure and thus closely relate to the specific plight of the Joads. For example, Chapter 3 described the never-say-die land turtle: the Joads have a turtle-like persistence and will soon be creeping southwest like the turtle. Chapter 7 described used-car lot activity: Tom's first home sight was of the second-hand Hudson which would take the Joads west. And so with Chapters 1, 5, 9, and several later ones. Steinbeck makes the Joads a microcosm, while his interchapters expressionistically sketch the vast socio-economic situation of which they are a part.

From the Critics

"Scattered through the sixteen interchapters are occasional paragraphs whose purpose is to present, with choric effect, the philosophy or social message to which the current situation gives rise. For the most part, these paragraphs occur in four chapters—9, 11, 14, and 19." [23]

Chapter 10 Summary

While the others are off selling family household effects and tools, Tom moons about the land. Ma says she hopes

---

[23]Lisca, *Wide World of Steinbeck*, p. 156.

that California will be nice. She mentions having seen handbills from California advertising for farm workers. She expresses the hope that the family may ultimately live in a little white house. Tom says that they should not plan too far ahead and then adds that in prison he heard that unemployment in California was up, wages were down, and migrant workers hived together in dirty camps.

Grampa tears in, jabbering, and Ma holds him and buttons his fly. Casy explains that he is finished as a preacher and will not seek to learn from others and will not pretend to teach them.

The truck returns. The men are glum, having been cheated. They sold everything to a smooth dealer for eighteen dollars. Rose of Sharon is along. She greets her brother Tom and smiles in the wonder of her pregnancy, which she takes very seriously. Tom casually shakes hands with Connie Rivers, her rather quiet husband. Ruthie and Winfield bounce off the truck, their mouths black with licorice whips.

In the evening a family council convenes. The men wonder how they can permit Casy to join such an already crowded group going west. The old Hudson will have to hold a dozen people as it is. But Ma says, "It ain't kin we? It's will we? . . . As far as 'kin,' we can't do nothin', not go to California or nothin'; but as far as 'will,' why, we'll do what we will." Casy joins the group, most gratefully, and his admiration for Ma grows.

They all pitch in and slaughter and scald and scrape their pigs, hang them briefly, and then cut and salt down the meat. First they plan to pack the next day and start west two mornings hence. But Tom suggests that they pack all night and leave at dawn. Ma carefully salts down the pork until Casy volunteers. Then she sorts through her meager papers and other belongings, saves a few precious mementoes, and reverently burns the rest in the cook stove. Rose of Sharon packs all their clothes. Al takes charge of loading the car. They level their boxes and tools, pile mattresses above, and rig a tarpaulin on top. Everyone but the grandparents and the young children work through the night.

At dawn the dogs bark at Muley Graves, who suddenly turns up to say goodbye. The Joads offer to make room for him, but he says that he will stay and haunt his home land "like a damn ol' graveyard ghos'." Suddenly Grampa refuses to leave his ancestral land and has to be drugged with soothing syrup and gently hoisted aboard. They take one dog, leave the others and the chickens to Muley, and drive slowly through the curling dust to the highway near Sallisaw. Ma looks straight ahead, with a great weariness in her eyes.

Commentary

After giving a kind of Homeric catalogue of equipment needed for the trip, Steinbeck launches his Okie Odyssey. A few significant features of this chapter should be pointed out. When Casy offers to help Ma with the pork, she protests that it is woman's work, to which he replies that there is too much work to divide it into men's work and women's. This comment reinforces a major theme in the novel: we must forget traditional rules and work hard to help each other. Next, when Muley asks Tom whether he intends to leave the state and thus violate his parole, Tom does not answer: later his presence in the migrating group will represent a physical help but an emotional strain and an actual danger. Finally, Grampa's reluctance to leave his home reminds us of the earlier general question: "How can we live without our lives?" (Chapter 9). Grampa is unconscious at departure time. Psychologically, he has started to die. It would be comforting to say that Rose of Sharon's unborn child will be his replacement in the great cycle of movement and change, but such is not to be the case.

From the Critics

"Ma Joad's daughter [Rose of Sharon] throughout the early part of the novel appears as a frivolous, self-centered adolescent creature, full of complaints and fears for herself and the child she carries in her womb." [24]

"First of all, the Joads travel in a covered wagon. True, it is an improvised truck, but Steinbeck very carefully calls attention to the rigging up of a tarpaulin cover to enclose the family living-space in the rear. Moreover, this wreck of an automobile is in such bad shape that one hardly thinks of it as machinery. Certainly the Joads do not. They regard it with affection and concern, and they minister to its needs till it becomes a living thing, a member of the family. The truck is both their covered wagon and their ox team." [25]

"The United States Employment Service is authority for the fact that no effort was made by any California farm group to bring labor here, by advertising or any other means. The farmers neither needed nor wanted additional workers, nor did they want the tax cost of supporting unneeded migrant workers." [26]

"*The Grapes of Wrath* is divided into thirty consecutive chapters with no larger grouping, but even a cursory reading reveals that the novel is made up of three major parts: the drought, the journey, and California. The first section ends with Chapter 10. It is separated from the second section, the journey, by *two* interchapters." [27]

---

[24]Watt, *Steinbeck,* p. 73.

[25]Bowron, "*The Grapes of Wrath*: A 'Wagons West' Romance," p. 87.

[26]Thos. W. McManus, "California Citizens Association Report," July 1, 1939, quoted in Marshall V. Hartranft, *Grapes of Gladness* (Los Angeles: De Vorss, 1939), p. 125.

[27]Lisca, *Wide World of Steinbeck,* p. 168.

Chapter 11   Summary

When people leave their hand-tilled land and when tractor men with nitrates not of the land replace them, the land is no longer something personal. When people abandon their houses, then bats, mice, owls, cats, and weeds take over. Soon the wind picks off shingles, and the houses begin to fall apart.

Commentary

This short chapter tells what happens when the delicate balance of human beings, their land, and their homes is wrenched. Vacating the houses makes the land vacant. The area is like sterile places in T. S. Eliot's *Waste Land,* and Grampa is a little like the wounded Fisher King.

Chapter 12   Summary

Highway 66 is "the mother road, the road of flight," into which a quarter of a million migrants in fifty thousand wounded, gasping, dying cars pour on their way west. The highway stretches from Sallisaw, Oklahoma, to Bakersfield, California. It is a terrifying trek, but at the end will be a paradise of valleys, orchards, vineyards, little houses, and jobs. The migrants are warned along the way that they will encounter trouble out west, but they stream on. Their cars rattle, blow gaskets, have flats, break fan belts, hiss steam. Part dealers cheat them. But they help each other on to California.

Commentary

For the first time, Steinbeck here gives us an intercalary chapter without a narrative chapter preceding it. Chapter 11 was a symbolic farewell to Oklahoma. Chapter 12, which does not mention the Joads, is the beginning of a new structural unit, roughly the second third of the novel. Thousands of homeless people are moving west in shuddering jalopies, and the Joads will add themselves to this river of human misery and courage.

From the Critics

"The great movement of the Okies across the dustbowl and into the Promised Land of California suggests the biblical analogy of the Chosen People fleeing into Israel. The story is shaped in heroic dimensions, and like the great epics of the past it is laid out over the face of the nation whose struggle it depicts. America struggling with the Depression, struggling for very life, is epic. The Joads are heroes specified among a whole people at war, hurling themselves against the armies of finance and fear. The conflict is not personal but national—which is the essence of the epic spirit." [28]

Chapter 13   Summary

The Hudson, with eleven Joads, Casy, and Rose of Sharon's husband Connie, is creaking over Highway 66. Al is purposefully at the wheel. He is "the soul of the car." When he questions Ma about their future, she says that she fears inactivity and that she is simply trying to live ahead a trifle at a time. "That's all I can do. I can't do no more. All the rest'd get upset if I done any more'n that."

After several slow hours, they stop near Paden, Oklahoma, for water and gas. The service-station owner is

---

[28]Walcutt, *American Literary Naturalism*, p. 263.

suspicious until they explain that they can buy gas and do not intend to trade shoes or dolls for it. Mentioning the hordes of migrants on the road, the owner wonders what the country is coming to. Tom and Casy talk with him briefly. The Joad dog laps some muddy water, wanders to the highway, and is instantly killed by a squealing car that speeds on at once. Winfield bravely looks at his mangled pet, then vomits. Rose of Sharon whines and expresses the hope that the incident will not taint her baby. Granma goes into the toilet, which has running water, and takes a nap inside. Grampa is still groggy. Soon they reassemble, and Tom takes a turn driving.

They go on and on, through Oklahoma City carefully and then past Bethany at twilight. Tom tells Ma that he will be in no danger through breaking his parole unless he commits a crime in California, but she is still worried. They stop by a culvert, where another car, a Dodge, is stalled, with a tent beside it. Ivy and Sairy Wilson, from Kansas, bid them welcome. The Joads boil down off their truck, and Grampa is suddenly very sick. He begins to cry. Sairy leads him into her tent, where he is watched over by Casy and uncomprehending Granma, who yells at Casy, "Pray, goddamn you!" Grampa is quickly worse. He gags, wheezes, has a stroke, and soon dies. The sun sets. Huge Diesel trucks pound past. And, we read, "The family became a unit."

Pa, head of the family now, takes charge, knows that they must bury Grampa at once, since they cannot afford any alternative. Tom suggests that they bury a bottle too, with a note explaining the facts of the old man's death. Letting Sairy and Rose of Sharon prepare a supper of Joad pork and Wilson potatoes, Ma lays Grampa out in Mrs. Wilson's quilt, on which he died. In her lovely low voice, Sairy explains that she is happy to be needed: "We're proud to help. I ain't felt so—safe in a long time. People needs— to help." Ma wants a message from Psalms, which will be written on a blank page from the Wilsons' Bible, buried with Grampa. The men dig the grave fast and deep. Again fearful that her baby may be harmed, Rose of Sharon is timid about joining the group while Casy offers his curious prayer. He says that Grampa is on an easy path now; therefore he will pray for people who "don' know which way to turn." His philosophy is that "All that lives is holy." Ruthie and Winfield are horrified and tearful. The men gently cover the quilted corpse, and then level the grave and strew dry grass over it to prevent detection.

They all eat supper. Granma lies whimpering on a mattress, and Ma sends Rose of Sharon over to lie beside her for comfort. Soon the two are whispering. When Wilson describes the ailments of his car, Al volunteers to fix what he diagnoses as a plugged gas line. The men talk about probable labor conditions in California. Then Tom and Al suggest sharing loads with the Wilsons and keeping together on the road; in that way, they can all get west. Everyone is delighted, except Sairy, who has been sick, is afraid of a relapse, and refuses to be a burden on others. Ma reassures her. Then they all sleep as the night noises rise about them —all but Sairy, who stares at the stars in pain.

Commentary

This is a pivotal narrative chapter. The Odyssey has started. The dog, unused to the strange environment of the highway, strayed and was killed. Then Grampa sickened and died. Like the dog which knew only the open spaces, Grampa could not be uprooted from his homeland. Pa's touching, inarticulate farewell to his father's body and Casy's Emersonian prayer for the living rather than for the dead are notable, as is the dramatic entrance of the Wilsons, who in needing help and giving it actually increase the courage of the remaining Joads, especially Ma, their tower of strength.

From the Critics

"Thirteen persons started west, Casy and twelve Joads, who . . . also represent Judea (Judah) whom Jesus came to teach. Not only were two Joads named Thomas, but another was John; Casy's name was James, brother and disciple of Jesus. One of the twelve, Connie Rivers, was not really a Joad; he is Judas, for not only did he desert the Joads selfishly at a critical moment [Chapter 20], but just before he did so he told his wife that he would have done better to stay home 'an' study 'bout tractors [to betray his friends with].' " [29]

" . . . [T]he epitaph which is buried with Grampa . . . is written on a page torn from the Wilsons' Bible—that page usually reserved for family records of births, marriages, and deaths. In burying this page with Grampa, the Wilsons symbolize not only their adoption of the Joads, but their renouncing of hope for continuing their own family line." [30]

"The sense of a communal unit grows steadily through the narrative—the Wilsons, the Wainwrights [Chapter 28]—and is pointed to again and again in the interchapters . . ." [31]

Chapter 14   Summary

Now comes a short lecture on psychology and economics. The western states are afraid of the Okie migration. The landowners there are fighting against government interference, increased social unity — which Steinbeck calls Manself—and higher taxes, not realizing that they are hitting at results, not the cause. The cause is hunger, and the frustration of men and women who—uniquely among organisms—

[29]Fontenrose, *Steinbeck*, p. 78.

[30]Lisca, *Wide World of Steinbeck*, p. 173.

[31]Lisca, *Wide World of Steinbeck*, p. 172.

want to progress. The thing the landowners should fear is the change from one evicted tenant's statement, "I lost my land," to the statement of two men and their families, then many, all camping together—"We lost *our* land." When "I have a little food" plus "I have none" adds up to "We have a little food," the sum is dangerous to the selfish landowner.

Commentary

This interchapter is Janus-like: the Joads and the Wilsons have just illustrated (in Chapter 13) the miraculous potency of united human endeavor. Then labor organizations in California (Chapters 24 and 26) will illustrate it on a more militant level.

From the Critics

"Here let me lay my cards on the table. About such a passage as this [on Manself] I have a divided feeling, as I do about some of the quietly eloquent sayings of Tom to his mother when he leaves her to take up the cause of labor [Chapter 28]. These statements of Tom about his mission, these statements of Steinbeck about Manself, do not seem to me among the best things in the book, considered as literary art; and yet I do not see how we could dispense with them. . . . But they do not seem to me altogether successful as imaginative shapings of the stuff of life in keeping with the most rigorous demands of fictional art." [32]

Chapter 15   Summary

This chapter is a dramatic vignette (sometimes separately reprinted as "Two-a-Penny"), unrelated to the Joads'

---

[32]Beach, *American Fiction*, p. 340.

story except thematically. At one of the innumerable hamburger stands along Highway 66—this one run by Mae and Joe—truckers and drivers of a variety of passenger cars stop. Dessicated ladies, wrinkled and weary, with bags of ointments and pills, get out, and so do the fat little businessmen with them. They spend little, drop paper napkins wastefully used, complain, and drive on. Mae calls them "shitheels." But the truckers, who regard her as "a ol' war horse," delight her, with their banter, their generosity, and their fundamental morality.

While two truckers are having a bite and a rest, a farmer with his family pulls up in a junk-piled wreck of a car. He asks for water, and while his two tow-headed boys stare—with wonder but no desire—at some candy, he asks to buy a dime's worth of bread. Mae wants to sell him sandwiches, which, however, he cannot afford. Al growls at her to give the farmer the fifteen-cent loaf for a dime. With a spare penny, the man wants to buy his boys a bit of striped peppermint. Though the pieces are a nickel each, Mae sells two of them for a penny to the boys, who march out, ecstatic, and then jump into the old car like chipmunks. The two truckers query Mae, who acts tough; but they understand and leave sizable tips.

Then Al casually plays one of his three slot-machines—the one which the truckers have been feeding the most—and on the fifth try hits the jack-pot.

Commentary

Steinbeck's sarcastic, broad-stroke sketch of the effete, complaining rich in their huge automobiles is devastating (if unfair). The quick scene in which two little children are treated to some unexpected candy is heart-rending. And by insisting on the generosity of the average truck driver,

Steinbeck seems to be trying to set the record straight, since Chapter 2 showed us an abnormal truck driver. The moral of this chapter, which is the longest of the intercalary units, is the simple golden rule.

From the Critics

"Chapter Fifteen . . . exemplifies Steinbeck's keen observation of the surface details of contemporary life and his sure grasp of the idiom of the common people." [33]

"The roadside hamburger stand is as finally and definitively done in Chapter Fifteen as is the train ride in Wolfe's *Of Time and the River*." [34]

"The vignette called 'Two-a-Penny' is another wonderfully wrought picture, a short story as tender, warm, and at the same time charged with bitterness, as any story in our literature. Only a man of great heart and good will could have written such a restrained and beautiful fragment." [35]

Chapter 16   Summary

The Joads and the Wilsons drive through the Texas Panhandle and into New Mexico past Santa Rosa. Then the Wilson car burns out a connecting-rod bearing. Rose of Sharon has been troubling Ma by her dream of Connie's getting a job as a radio-man in a town. Ma wants the family to stick together. So when Tom suggests that he and Casy remain behind and repair the Wilson car while the others

---

[33]Walter Blair, Theodore Hornberger, and Randall Stewart, *The Literature of the United States*, 2 vols. (Chicago: Scott, Foresman, 1953), II, 1150.

[34]Fontenrose, *Steinbeck*, p. 70.

[35]George Snell, *The Shapers of American Fiction: 1798-1947* (New York: Dutton, 1947), p. 195.

go ahead, in the hope of getting jobs and laying some money aside, Ma grabs a jack handle and threatens to fight Pa. Surrendering, Pa says helplessly, "She sassy." Ma's argument goes as follows: "What we got lef' in the worl'? Nothin' but us. Nothin' but the folks. . . . All we got is the family unbroke." Ma wins.

So Al drives ahead with the others to find a camp site, while Tom and Casy take out the defective connecting-rod. Tom cuts his hand but stops the bleeding with mud and urine. Casy verbosely ponders their uncertain future in California, until Tom tells him that the best procedure is simply to put one foot down and then the other, and to proceed that way. Al returns, reports that the family is camped at a place for fifty cents and that Granma is delirious now. Then Al gives the other two men some food which Ma sent. "She don't forget nobody," says Casy admiringly.

While Casy guards the Wilson car, Tom and Al drive the Hudson to a junk-yard to look for parts. Al first talks about prostitutes and then asks Tom to describe prison life; but Tom refuses, saying that the mere thought of it makes his guts "all droopy and nasty feelin'." Soon they are talking with a morose, one-eyed junk-man who bitterly reviles his absent boss and therefore gives them a good price on the rod, a flashlight, and some socket wrenches. As they return to the other car, Al praises Tom for telling the one-eyed man to stop feeling sorry for himself. Tom urges Al not to think that anyone is blaming him for the burned-out bearing—". . . don't keep ya guard up when nobody ain't sparrin' with ya. You gonna be all right." When Al says that he might try to take some correspondence-school course in radio, TV, or auto repair work, as Connie is thinking of doing, Tom advises him to learn what the cost will be first and be prepared to stick it out in spite of discouragements.

They are lucky to be able to repair the Wilson Dodge, in the dark but with their flashlight. Al commends Tom, and

Casy says that he could never repair a car even after watching the others do so. Tom has learned about mechanics in prison. The three drive the Hudson and the Dodge on ahead to the camp site.

The proprietor of the place refuses to let the second car in without a second half-dollar payment. Tom almost fights the man for calling him a bum but decides instead to drive ahead and sleep in the ditch until the caravan can start again in the morning. A ragged man warns the Joad men that some California landowners have printed more posters, asking for workers, than there are jobs available. He learned the hard way, by going west and losing his wife and two children to death by starvation, before he decided to return home. Tom talks briefly with Ma and keeps Pa from telling her what the ragged man said. Then, walking past the proprietor and hurling a clod at his wooden house, Tom goes on ahead. Granma is becoming sicker and is now "nimsy-mimsy."

Commentary

The unity of the group is being further threatened in this chapter, by the break-down of Wilson's Dodge, by the unfriendly camp proprietor—who through need for money contributes to a brief symbolic split of Tom away from the others—and by Granma's worsening condition. Characterization of Al is deepened through action and dialogue. The ragged man is a prophet of future doom, like Elijah in Melville's *Moby Dick*. The ragged man's description of the typical farm boss's hiring technique will prove accurate (in Chapter 26): "The more fellas he can get, an' the hungrier, less he's gonna pay." Here also, Steinbeck reinforces his fixed notion that ownership breeds selfish indifference to others: the one-eyed man hates his boss, and the camp owner is portrayed as a victimizer of itinerant "bums" moving past him to the West. On the other hand, a strange woman cooking beans at the camp offers Tom a plate if he will come back at daybreak.

From the Critics

" . . . Ma takes over, surprising herself as much as her men-folk by her new stature—which she achieves (as all 'Wagons West' leaders must) by forcibly taking charge in a situation threatening the cohesion and safety of the new wagon-train society. Ma Joad, brandishing her jackhandle at Pa, is an archetypical character." [36]

Chapter 17   Summary

This interchapter tells of the temporary worlds which are created by twenty or so families each night at the camp sites. These little worlds have their leaders, laws, rules of etiquette, and rituals for establishing relationships, all of which are for the health, protection, and happiness of the people. A world is built each night, and it is torn down at daybreak. After supper, usually prepared in accordance with an unstated pattern, social groups form to talk of the past and the future, to make music, and to listen and rest.

Commentary

These men, women, and children may break written laws and offend the authorities, but they are developing an unwritten code which is both necessary and operative. So they should not be called lawless. They punish wrongdoers instantly, by fights or ostracism. They instinctively protect

---

[36]Bowron, *The Grapes of Wrath*: A 'Wagons West' Romance," p. 89.

with special care the pregnant and the sick. Earlier Casy said, "Law changes, . . . but 'got to's' go on. You got the right to do what you got to do" (Chapter 13). This chapter dramatizes the truth of his statement.

Chapter 18   Summary

The Joads and the Wilsons drive on, through the upland of New Mexico and into the high country of Arizona near the Painted Desert. A guard stops them and warns them to keep moving. They go past Flagstaff and Topock and into eastern California. They stop by a cool stream, and the men bathe. They have forty dollars left and are apprehensive about the desert ahead of them. Two men come up to swim. They are father and son, and they tell a grim story about working conditions in California, which they are leaving to return to the Panhandle. California has lush fruit lands but often they are unworked and are patrolled by armed guards. The deputies call the migrants Okies: " . . . Okie use' ta mean you was from Oklahoma. Now it means you're a dirty son-of-a-bitch."

The Joads are worried but rest and plan to go on. The man tells his son that he should not have talked to them the way he did, that nothing can dissuade them from going, and that now they are only miserable before they have to be.

Suddenly Noah tells Tom that he cannot go any farther, that he loves the little river and must stay there. He adds that his folks do not really care for him. Although Tom swears and argues, Noah walks away and disappears in the willows by the water.

Granma is sicker, and Ma and Rose of Sharon fan her as she deliriously scolds Grampa, whom she imagines to be still among them. Ma gently tells her daughter that birth pangs and death pangs are all part of a continuous pattern of natural change. A religious fanatic enters the tent and insists upon conducting a prayer and hymn meeting for Granma. Ma drives the woman out, but then the ensuing sing-song chant rises outside anyway, and sounds like the wail and cry of beasts. When Granma seems less fretful, Ma is sorry that she was rude to the fanatic. Suddenly a trooper in khaki and boots bursts in and warns Ma to move on quickly. He calls her an Okie. As he leaves, Ma turns black with rage.

Tom awakens, bathes again, is called by Ruthie to Ma, and learns about the policeman. He tells her that Noah is gone. She is silent, then says, "Family's fallin' apart. . . . I jus' can't think. They's too much." Pa blames himself for Noah's strangeness and now his disappearance.

The Joads have to separate from the Wilsons, since Sairy is now too sick to go on. She begs Casy to recite a prayer. He thinks through one silently, and Sairy is relieved a bit and tells him in her beautifully low voice that she is dying. The Joads load their truck, and the group of eleven people prepare to leave the Wilsons. Ma has Pa give the Wilsons two dollars and some meat. When Wilson refuses and threatens to become angry, Ma gently places the gifts in front of their tent.

The Joads stop at Needles for gas, oil, water, and a map. The service-station attendants admire their nerve but criticize them for being sub-human as they lumber out for the desert.

The epic drive across the desert begins. Tom is at the wheel. Uncle John tells Casy about his wife's death and his fear that he is a sinful jinx on all people now. Ma is lying beside Granma on the back of the truck. When the sick old woman croaks out a complaint, Ma says gently, "You know the family got to get acrost." When Ruthie and Winfield fall asleep, Connie and Rose of Sharon furtively make love. At Daggett about midnight they are stopped by agricultural inspectors, but Ma tells them that Granma is terribly sick and hysterically begs not to be forced to unpack and prove that they are not carrying any vegetables or seeds. They are allowed to drive on. Later Tom stops for gas, and then Al drives. At dawn they pass through Mojavi and then Tehachapi.

Suddenly Al slams on the brakes, and everyone awakens to look down on the lush green valley below, with orchards and groves, houses and rich barns. Their joy is shattered, however, when Ma announces that Granma is dead, and was before they got to Daggett. Pa wishes that his mother had lived to see California. Tom is moved by his mother's formidable strength. Ma had to make sure that the family kept going through the night. Casy says of her in wonder, "John, there's a woman so great with love—she scares me." Ruthie and Winfield are appalled by the stiff little corpse under its pink curtain. Rose of Sharon and Connie recall in whispers what they were doing while Granma was dying.

Commentary

The Colorado River provides an ironic baptism for the Joads at the beginning of this chapter. There they are told the meaning of the term Okie. There Sairy Wilson prepares to die. There Noah splits away from his family. And there the trooper tells the Joads to keep moving. The service-station men's comments that the Okies are more like gorillas than human beings is bitterly ironic in the light of the almost unbearable human drama of Granma's dying shortly thereafter. Casy's philosophizing continues, and his theories will find pragmatic sanction in the course of the next chapters. Ma remains a pillar of strength. Tom and Casy realize what she must have endured when she lay with a corpse through the sleepless night so that her family could get to the paradise-like valley. At exactly the half-way mark of the novel, in number of pages, the Joads first see the valley in which they hope to make a new home.

From the Critics

"Noah, a modern Ishmael who symbolizes the loneliness of man's spirit, departs to find his own Eden along the river which flows through the barren desert—one more of Steinbeck's interesting juxtapositions of life and death elements with water." [37]

"Granma died in the night that followed their arrival in California. The new venture is not for the ancestors; but the pauper's grave that Granma received in California [in Chapter 20] links the old country [Oklahoma, where Grampa is buried] to the new and the Joad family to another land: this is now their home." [38]

"For a moment, when the Joad caravan laboriously tops its last mountain pass and gazes out over the incredibly beautiful, fruitful valley of its dreams, the West has been won. . . . Steinbeck's prose at this point achieves Hollywood lushness as he labors to produce a heightened composite image of Everyman's vision of the Garden of the West." [39]

"The journey section extends past the geographical California border, across the desert to Bakersfield. This section ends with Chapter 18, . . . and the next chapter begins the California section by introducing the reader to labor conditions in that state." [40]

---

[37]H. Kelly Crockett, "The Bible and *The Grapes of Wrath,*" *College English,* XXIV (December, 1962), 197.

[38]Fontenrose, *Steinbeck,* p. 82.

[39]Bowron, *"The Grapes of Wrath*: A 'Wagons West' Romance," p. 90.

[40]Lisca, *Wide World of Steinbeck,* pp. 168-169.

Chapter 19   Summary

California once belonged to Mexico, until hordes of tattered Americans poured into it to squat on the land, dispossess the earlier occupants, and claim it by living there for a couple of generations. Then the farmers gradually became like shopkeepers, manufacturing their produce rather than personally growing it, hiring imported Oriental and Mexican labor at low wages, concentrating on fruit and vegetables instead of grain, and farming "on paper." In time, the workers were in debt to the fewer and fewer big fat owners.

But the Okies are somewhat different. They are Americans, and they are pouring in by the tens of thousands into California, saying that "a fallow field is a sin and the unused land a crime against the thin children." They establish Hoovervilles, rotten sprawling camps of houses made from corrugated cardboard. which melts in the rain. The wary owners force wages down, hire and arm deputies to patrol their land and keep Okies moving about, and constantly fear the day when the migrants will organize and make a stand. Thus the owners, fighting conditions rather than causes, forget three principles: when too few men are owners, their land will be taken away from them; most hungry and cold people will resort to violence; and repression only knits the poor people more closely together.

Commentary

This chapter on history and economics ushers in the second half of the novel. The Joads are now in California. Their observations of the conditions just indicated will next be dramatized on a personal level. The truth of the implicit prediction of violence and coming labor organization will be borne out in succeeding chapters as the fate of the Joads unfolds.

From the Critics

"The human erosion pictured in the book is as much the result of a separation from the land as it is of poverty. And because for the absentee growers their land has become a column of figures in a book, they too are suffering an erosion —a moral one. [Thomas] Jefferson would have had no difficulty understanding what Steinbeck was getting at . . ." [41]

Chapter 20   Summary

The Joad family goes to the coroner at Bakersfield to leave Granma's body to be buried in potter's field with a five-dollar wooden marker. Ma is terribly dejected. They drive back to a camp and soon unpack their belongings for the time being. Tom strikes up a conversation with a young fellow grinding the valves of his ancient Buick. They talk, and the stranger advises Tom to act "bull-simple" in front of the roving police, whose strategy is to raid the splintery Hoovervilles periodically and thus keep the migrants from getting organized. The fellow adds that the police regularly jail the leaders and then blacklist them. Tom returns to his unit and commends Al for the good condition of their Hudson. When Casy slowly suggests that he should move off and thus make one less mouth for Ma to feed, Tom says that he senses something about to explode — ex-convicts get "sensy" — and that Casy ought to stay a while.

Connie is sitting beside Rose of Sharon, who is sick. When he complains about the squalor of the camp, Rose of

[41]Lisca, *Wide World of Steinbeck*, pp. 153-154.

Sharon urges him to keep thinking of radio repair work. Meanwhile Ma is cooking a thin stew over a twig fire, and a crowd of about fifteen hungry children drifts around her. One little girl speaks wistfully of a government camp to the south where she and her folks stayed: it had flush toilets, warm-water showers, and music at night. Now it is full, however, and they cannot return there.

Al is attracted to the old Buick nearby. He strikes up a conversation with Floyd Knowles, the young man grinding the valves. Al helps Floyd, who tells him how several men get together, tour around in one car looking for work, and thus save gas.

When Ma dishes up the stew, Uncle John claims he is not hungry. Tom orders him to eat. Ma tells the swarm of hungry children to find flat sticks and scoop what is left from the nearly empty pot. It grieves her not to share; yet she does not have enough food for her immediate family. A tough woman comes up and starts to criticize Ma for feeding strange children and thus making them discontent with their regular diet. Ma asks the woman to sit down and explain matters. The woman drops her eyes and soon walks away.

Al excitedly comes for Tom, and they go to Floyd, who tells them that there is absolutely no work here and that he has just heard of work in the Santa Clara Valley two hundred miles north. Tom is reluctant to think of moving so soon. Al is tempted to break off from the family and hitch-hike north for work and money, but Tom tells him that Ma would be displeased.

Suddenly a labor contractor in a new Chevrolet drives in, with a deputy at his side, to hire men for work at Tulare. When he refuses to specify the number of men or the wages, Floyd angrily criticizes him. The deputy with a cold smile starts to arrest him on a trumped-up charge and calls him a red agitator. Floyd slugs the deputy, who staggers while

Tom impulsively trips him. He shoots after Floyd, who is running toward the willows. A woman screams, her knuckles on one hand sliced off by the .45 bullet. Casy rushes up, seeing the deputy aiming again, and kicks him in the neck. He falls unconscious, as the contractor speeds off in the Chevvy. Casy tells Tom to hide, since he is already a parole violator, and tells Al to stay out of the whole affair. When the police arrive, Casy takes all the blame. The deputy is unable to identify anyone clearly; so they take proud Casy away.

As Al emerges from the Joad tent to go get Tom, Uncle John confesses that he held back five dollars to get drunk on. Now Casy's act of self-sacrifice has disturbed his conscience. Pa takes the five dollars but gives him two dollars back again, and off goes Uncle John for his bottle. Then Al and Tom return, and it is revealed that Connie has walked up the river and is not coming back. Pa says that Connie never was any good. Ma dislikes such criticism and prefers to think of her defecting son-in-law as dead. Meanwhile Ruthie and Winfield are outside, staggering in imitation of the way Uncle John acts when he is drunk. Tom goes after him, since the family must quickly eat and drive off before the deputy and his cronies return to burn out the camp, as they have grimly promised to do.

Tom learns from the storekeeper what ditch to seek Uncle John in and goes on until he finds the drunken fellow. When Uncle John refuses to return to the clan, Tom carefully knocks him out and carries him back to the truck. Rose of Sharon does not want to abandon the hope of reuniting with Connie, but Tom explains that he has left word at the store for Connie that the Joads would be going south. Just before they pile in and drive off, Tom orders Al to ride up back and to keep hold of their big monkey wrench in case the authorities try to stop them. He places Ma in the middle of the front seat and Pa, armed with the jack handle, to her right. Tom drives. When Ma complains that he is getting mean, he replies, "They're tryin' to break us. . . . They're workin' on our decency." He knows that the vicious deputies, who are about to burn the camp, are hardly the law.

After a little driving through the darkness, they are stopped by some deputies with lanterns and shotguns. Tom tenses but then whiningly asks how to get to Tulare. They are let through. Soon Tom stops, turns off the lights and motor, and watches the armed mob proceed to the Hooverville and set it afire. Then Tom returns to the other Joads and announces that he thinks they should all drive south to the government camp at Weedpatch, not north to Tulare.

Ma commends his restraint, but Tom says that he is losing his self-respect, to which she replies significantly, "You got to have patience. Why, Tom—us people will go on livin' when all them people is gone. Why, Tom, we're the people that live. They ain't gonna wipe us out. Why, we're the people—we go on."

They drive on through side streets of the town and then turn south on Highway 99.

Commentary

This chapter is the longest and most melodramatic in the novel thus far. It begins in despair, continues through frustration, then includes violence, and ends with the escape of the Joads. Contrasting events are the desertion of Rose of Sharon by her husband Connie and Jim Casy's self-sacrifice for Tom. The kind of home the Joads can expect in California is quickly shown them: one Hooverville after another. The kind of cooperation necessary for the migrants to survive the brutality of the authorities is also demonstrated: when Al helps Floyd, that young man in return tells the Joads that there may be work to the north. A kind of naturalistic determinism operates in this chapter, and indeed in the whole novel: even though Floyd warns Tom to act "bull-simple" (that is, numbed by police pushing) because the authorities arrest any potential Hooverville leaders, Floyd himself queries the labor contractor so keenly that the deputy tries to arrest him as a "red." Further, Uncle John cracks under the pressure of Casy's phenomenal goodness. Tom shows signs of incipient violence. He trips one deputy and wants to take a monkey wrench to another. Only Ma continues to be the same, a pillar of unifying strength for the family. It is she who voices the Carl Sandburg-like faith in the people.

From the Critics

". . . [T]he disappearance of Rose of Sharon's husband, Connie Rivers . . . is especially an affront to tradition, both because the young people have already threatened the family's security with talk of striking out for themselves . . . and because, by Connie's defection, a potential family unit is shattered as it is forming." [42]

Chapter 21   Summary

The migrants are becoming desperate. They have come from a pre-industrial way of life, and the ways of industry seem ridiculous to them. The owners out west band together, hire agents and spies and blacklisters, and convince themselves that Okies are ignorant, dirty, and even degenerate. Meanwhile, the big farmers buy canneries, force fruit prices down, keep the price of canned produce high, and thus

---

[42]Warren French, *John Steinbeck* (New York: Twayne, 1961), p. 104.

squeeze out the small farmers, who then become migrants themselves. "And the anger began to ferment."

Commentary

Like Chapters 19 and 25, this intercalary chapter is a lesson in California land ownership and the dangers inherent in the capitalistic system. As such, this chapter presents the huge economic and social backdrop against which the Joad family tragedy can be enacted.

From the Critics

"[T]he central message of *The Grapes of Wrath* is an appeal to the owning class to behave, to become enlightened, rather than to the working class to change its own condition." [43]

Chapter 22   Summary

Tom finds the government camp at Weedpatch, California, and learns that there is a vacancy for one family. The eight Joads pile into it. Soon Tom is willingly answering certain necessary questions from the watchman, who explains some of the rules concerning sanitation, self-government through an elected central committee, dances, and the like. Tom is thrilled, returns to the truck and the tent already set up beside it, and hints to his suddenly girlish Ma that things are looking up.

In the morning Tom rises early, meets his neighbors— Timothy Wallace, his son Wilkie Wallace, and that young man's wife, who is cooking breakfast and nursing her baby

---

[43]Hyman, "Some Notes on John Steinbeck," p. 195.

at the same time. Tom shares their bread, bacon, and coffee with them as dawn breaks. The two men invite Tom to join them in laying pipe for Mr. Thomas, owner of a small farm nearby. Telling Ruthie to explain to Ma, Tom happily walks off with the Wallaces, who recently had to sell their car for $10 and then saw it on a used-car lot priced at $75.

Arriving at the farm, the three learn from Thomas that the Farmers' Association has threatened him with foreclosure unless he brings down the wage for pipe-laying from thirty to twenty-five cents an hour. He further warns the men that the authorities are going to make trouble at the dance next Saturday night so as to have an excuse to raid and close the government camp. The authorities fear that the campers will soon organize and demand decent wages. Such agitators are called reds. Tom decides that he must be a red himself in that case. The three men start digging the long ditch for the pipe. Tom enjoys the feel of the pickaxe and swings it hard, grunting and sweating as he does so.

Meanwhile, back at the camp Ruthie gets Winfield up and takes him to the toilets, uses one, and then leaps high off it when he pushes the flusher by mistake. They think that the whole contraption is broken. They rush back to Ma, and Ruthie tells about Tom's job, then about the toilets. Ma goes over to inspect, laughs when Winfield flushes one again and is similarly frightened, and then looks about until a man comes in and tells her that she is in the men's side. More kindly, he then explains that the ladies' committee will call on her soon.

Now Ma is all bustle. She wakes up Pa, Uncle John, Al, and Rose of Sharon, tells them to clean up, and tries to get breakfast over with before the visit. Jim Rawley, the camp manager, strolls by and has a friendly cup of coffee with Ma at her tent opening. Ma is moved almost to tears by his genteel sincerity. The Joads eat fast. Then, while the men take the truck to look for work, Rose of Sharon comes back from the toilet to tell Ma that a woman there told her that camp nurses help pregnant women and that often the campers donate baby things after a birth. Rose of Sharon is very pleased.

Then a wild, religious woman, on her way to the laundry, sees Rose of Sharon and her condition, stops, and darkly criticizes morals in the camp. The woman describes a recent bloody stillbirth. She blames playacting and "clutch-an'-hug" dancing in camp. When she leaves, Rawley returns and tries to reassure Rose of Sharon by telling her that the woman is a meddling fanatic and that the only sins in camp are cold and hunger and overwork, which cause stillbirths.

Ma returns from a glorious shower-bath, and she and Rose of Sharon wonder whether Connie will ever reappear. When the girl says that sin may kill her child, Ma orders her to quit such thinking and get to work instead. The welcoming committee then appears, with Mrs. Jessie Bullitt in charge, and Mrs. Annie Littlefield and Mrs. Ella Summers with her. They take Ma and Rose of Sharon to the sanitary unit and explain the rules of cooperation and credit at the Weedpatch store. They distinguish nicely between credit and charity: credit is borrowing from a group of one's own kind, whereas charity is a gift which breaks one's spirit.

Ruthie and Winfield hang back, and then Ruthie interrupts a croquet game of some other children, who then walk off until the ostracized girl gets the point, drops the mallet, and runs home crying.

The committee leaves Ma feeling "perked up" happily. Rose of Sharon hopes to work in the nursery and thus learn how to care for babies. Ma hopes that the menfolk have found employment. When the religious fanatic returns, introduces herself as Lisbeth Sandry, and starts to lecture against dancing and hugging, Ma orders her away and threatens her with a piece of wood. Mrs. Sandry suddenly throws a fit and then begins to moan uncontrollably. Rawley walks by and asks some people to get her to her tent. Then he tells Ma that the woman is not well. But Rose of Sharon has been made wretched by her dire predictions. Ma comforts the girl but is saddened herself when Pa comes in and reports no work. Poor Ma begins to review their miseries: Grampa has died, Noah has walked off down the river, Granma has been buried as a pauper, and Connie has sneaked away. Ma and Pa talk about the pre-winter ducks flying over their Oklahoma home. Uncle John is disconsolate and fears that Tom has run off. Ma says that she is sure of Tom. "Ain't he a good boy!" Suddenly Ma wants Pa to go to the store and buy something nice for supper.

Commentary

This long chapter opens on a note of specious hope: the camp is friendly, and the Joads would like to make a home there for a while. Tom gets a temporary job. But in the offing is the possibility of trouble with the apprehensive authorities. Also Pa, Uncle John, and Al fail to find any employment. The car needs a tire. Rose of Sharon is afraid that her unborn baby is burning up within her. It seems inevitable that Tom's joy in hard, sweaty work will prove short-lived. Suspense mounts.

From the Critics

"The democracy, self-government, and fraternity of the roadside camps [in Chapter 17] blossomed more perfectly in the government camps, where men were orderly and harmonious without police. And the government camps, in which a minority of the migrants lived, were the model for the future commune of all workers." [44]

---

[44]Fontenrose, *Steinbeck,* p. 73.

"The one bright spot in the novel is the government camp, where the Joads find sanctuary for a while and show that they can live like decent human beings if given half a chance. But here again, in spite of Steinbeck's openly expressed bias against finance capitalism, he hardly conforms to the rest of the Marxian doctrine."[45]

"The trouble with the Weedpatch Camp is that it provides the migrants with everything but work. The dream of these migrants is not to be supported, but to work land of their own. Steinbeck is definitely no collectivist." [46]

". . . [Warren] French [*Steinbeck,* p. 99] prefers to interpret the scene involving the Joad children's unfamiliarity with flush toilets as evidence of Steinbeck's unsentimental and cool appraisal of the deficiencies and ignorance of his oppressed group, when it might as easily be read as a kind of primitive fun with overtones of pathos." [47]

"This bit of normal human activity, warmth, and tenderness [Tom's having breakfast with the Wallaces] is Tom's first experience in the refuge of the federal migrant camp, immediately following a night of vigilante horror and cringing flight. It constitutes for him a renewal of faith in his fellow man." [48]

"The book *could* have ended [but rightly does not] with the picture of life in Weedpatch, the government camp. This would have provided what I will call 'The New Deal' ending, familiar enough in the literature of the period and

[45]Rod W. Horton and Herbert W. Edwards, *Backgrounds of American Literary Thought* (New York: Appleton-Century-Crofts, 1952), p. 243.

[46]French, *Steinbeck,* p. 110.

[47]Jules Chametzky, "The Ambivalent Endings of *The Grapes of Wrath,*" *Modern Fiction Studies,* XI (Spring, 1965), p. 36. Reprinted with permission.

[48]Lisca, *Wide World of Steinbeck,* p. 176.

in such classic documentary films of the 'thirties as Pare Lorentz's 'The River' and 'The City.' " [49]

"The pattern of the novel . . . is similar to a parabola whose highest point is the sequence at the Government Camp. From Chapter XXII to the middle of Chapter XXVI, which covers this interlude, the animal imagery is almost totally absent." [50]

Chapter 23   Summary

How do the migrant people find pleasure? They gather around an old story-teller, who describes Indian fighting. One man might go to a movie and then return to camp and tell everyone else the whole strange plot. With a little spare money a man might get drunk and then lie on the soft ground and think of old times and of girls. Plenty of migrants can make music, and young couples stray off into the hay and their worried parents only momentarily try to stop them: ". . . might as well stop the sap from movin' in the trees." And preachers labor mightily in the ditches to baptize the sinners: "Take 'em, Christ!" And those baptized feel washed clean of all sin.

Commentary

This charming little chapter balances against Chapter 19 and 21 before it and Chapter 25 after it. Those other chapters are devoted to the rapacious landowners. Chapter 23 belongs to the people.

---

[49]Chametzky, "The Ambivalent Endings of *The Grapes of Wrath*," p. 37.

[50]Bluestone, *Novels into Film*, p. 151.

Chapter 24 Summary

On Saturday afternoon the scrubbing of the children begins. Then the weary men return and bathe. Ezra Huston, chairman of the central committee, calls a meeting and plans strategy to prevent violence at the evening dance. Willie Eaton, entertainment committee chairman, explains that he has increased the size of his group, and that they plan to surround any troublesome dancers quickly and get them out without bloodshed. They will not give the authorities any excuse to raid the camp.

The Joads eat their skimpy meal fast. Then Pa scrubs Ruthie and Winfield, at Ma's suggestion. Al spruces up and hopes to meet some pretty girls. Tom is on a committee. Ma talks Rose of Sharon into attending the dance in spite of her self-consciousness about her appearance. If any man asks her to dance, Ma will explain that the girl is feeling sick. She wants her daughter not to shame the family. Meanwhile Pa has begun to talk with a black-hatted man about accepting work at twenty cents an hour which Black Hat has been doing for twenty-five. Black Hat says that he would then do it for fifteen. They agree that the situation is bleak.

Tom is watching at the gate with Jule Vitela, who is half Cherokee Indian. Three nervous-looking men pass through the gate guard, saying that Jackson invited them to the dance. Jule checks with Jackson and learns that although he once worked with the three men he did not invite them. So the entertainment committeemen surround the would-be troublemakers, rebuke them bitterly for turning against their own kind simply for a bribe, and then spirit them over the back fence unharmed but warned.

The dance is a genuine pleasure for the young bucks, the blushing girls, and the onlooking parents and children—

but not for the "Jesus-lovers," the sanctimonious oldsters who regard hugging as a quick way to the devil.

Many of the older men are bunched together near the office, still talking about work. Black Hat says that once near Akron a rubber company hired some mountain men at cheap wages. But they joined a union. The storekeepers and "legioners" and preachers called the workers reds, and violent trouble seemed inevitable. So the mountain men, all with rifles, held an innocent turkey shoot outside town. In the process five thousand of them marched through town armed. There was never any more trouble. Black Hat says that perhaps the men in the Hoovervilles should organize a turkey-shooting club.

Commentary

Suspense continues to mount. An incident that might have been murderous was averted through the use of more restraint by the migrants than the owners or their deputies ever showed. This chapter also demonstrates the power of organization. Without it, the entertainment committee could not have prevented disaster. And Black Hat's grim suggestion concerning an organized show of force points to the kind of violence which will mark the bitter future.

Chapter 25 Summary

In the spring, California is fragrant with a sensual fulness. Skillful scientists have developed dozens of new fruits. The land is teeming with farm produce. But when harvesttime comes, the big canneries, owned by the big landowners, depress prices and force wholesale crop-dumping in spite of almost universal hunger. Then the small farmer is ruined. "Men who have created new fruits in the world cannot create a system whereby their fruits may be eaten." Oranges are piled high and sprayed with kerosene. Potatoes are dumped into the river. Pigs are slaughtered in ditches and buried in quicklime. And children die of malnutrition. And "in the eyes of the people there is the failure; and in the eyes of the hungry there is a growing wrath. In the souls of the people the grapes of wrath are filling and growing heavy, growing heavy for the vintage."

Commentary

This interchapter concludes the first half (Chapters 19-25) of the California section of the novel (Chapters 19-30). What began with promise, when the Joads entered the fertile California valley, now ends in bitter frustration. The migrants, who have practiced more restraint than the men of authority, may soon explode in violence. The grapes of wrath are filling.

From the Critics

"Chapter 25 begins as a glowing eulogy of the region's beauty and fertility. . . . This is the California the Joads have come to, a country about to reap a harvest of violence." [51]

"When, in Chapter Twenty-Five, he wishes to condemn the waste engendered by the profit motive, Steinbeck contrasts the callous burning of surplus foods with the labor, skill, and intelligence that went into producing it. In that context, the machine is an instrument of good . . . Here [in contrast to the tractors of Chapter 5] we see no discrepancy between technology and the natural process—

---

[51]Watt, *Steinbeck,* p. 69.

technology is simply a means of enhancing and, indeed, protecting it. The evil in this chapter is the profit motive . . ." [52]

"The reduction in acreage in all branches of agriculture and the necessary proration to keep the industry from disaster are such as to limit labor needs. The migration [from Oklahoma, Arkansas, Texas, and Missouri] came at the time when it was utterly impossible to give employment to additional workers without destroying the established farm economic system." [53]

Chapter 26   Summary

The Joads have now spent a month in the government camp at Weedpatch. Their supplies are very low. No work is available. The men are disconsolate. Ma announces that Winfield is sick, that Rose of Sharon is almost due to have her baby, and that therefore they must move out to seek work elsewhere. She roughly challenges Pa in order to make him threaten her and then smiles, saying to Tom, "He's all right. He ain't beat." Tom is her sole comfort and support. As she tells him, "Ever'thing you do is more'n you."

They prepare to leave. When Rose of Sharon complains, Ma pleases her with a present of some gold earrings and pierces the girl's ears with a needle and cork. Meanwhile Al strolls over to a girl friend to say goodbye. The girl is annoyed and says that she wants to get married. So he lightly asks her if she is pregnant. She is not. Al trips her, and they roll in the dry grass. He says that in about a month he will come back for her with his pockets jingling. Tom talks disconsolately with Willie Eaton and Jule Vitela about

[52]Chametzky, "The Ambivalent Endings of *The Grapes of Wrath*," p. 39.

[53]McManus, "California Citizens Association Report," quoted in Hartranft, *Grapes of Gladness,* p. 125.

forming a union for their protection and to keep wages up. Ruthie tells Ma that Winfield got into a fist fight with an Oregon boy who called the Joads Okies. Pa and Uncle John go over to the toilets to use them one last mournful time. Uncle John says that he feels a sin coming on.

Before dawn, Ma rouses the whole family. They load and leave, driving soon toward Bakersfield on Highway 99. Shortly after sun-up, they have a flat tire. While they are patching the tube, a pleasant-looking man drives up and tells them that there is work at the Hooper ranch forty miles north. They speed away, no longer bickering but instead building castles in the air. Ma hopes for a little house and a supply of food. Tom starts reminiscing about prison life, in spite of Ma's begging him to forget it. When they get near the ranch, they are puzzled by the sight of four policemen on motorcycles. They examine the Joads, escort them through a mob of jeering men, and take them along with the occupants of a few other recently arrived cars, into the enclosed ranch.

Soon the Joads are busy picking peaches at five cents a box. When Al begins to gripe, Pa bitterly rebukes him. At first they pick too fast and hence bruise the fruit. But soon the men settle steadily into the monotonous work. The children help. Later Ma comes out to pick, reporting as she does so that Rose of Sharon has fainted in the house assigned the Joads. When the children start to whine, Ma begs them to be good for now. Twenty big boxes later, Ma takes a credit slip to the store nearby and trades it for hamburger meat, potatoes, bread, and coffee. The timid little store-keeper, an employee of the ranch company, loans Ma a dime for sugar. She goes back to the house and cooks supper.

After dark, Tom says that he is curious about the crowd at the gate. Pa is too tired to do anything. Al wants to survey the area for girls. So Tom goes alone, eludes a menacing guard at the fence, and soon encounters some agitators, including Jim Casy. They are delighted to meet again. Casy is now a strike leader. He explains how some of his fellow-prisoners bellowed in unison against their diet of sour beans. Their united action got results. He warns Tom that when the deputies break up the strikers, the workers inside the barbed wire will be picking peaches for two and a half cents a box—a dollar a ton, picked and carried. Tom says that the Joads must have food, regardless of labor strategy. Casy praises the self-sacrificial nature of labor leaders.

Suddenly he is nervous. He and Tom and the others hurriedly leave the little tent where they have been talking, quietly go along a stream, and almost elude the deputies who are pursuing them. But then some flashlights seek them out. They stand still. A heavy deputy approaches Casy, who says that the tactics of the authorities are simply resulting in starvation to children. "You don' know what you're a-doin'," Casy manages to say. Then he is clubbed to death.

Tom wrenches the pick handle from the deputy and kills him with several crushing blows. Tom takes a heavy blow from a second policeman but escapes, runs, and hides in a thicket, gets back into the ranch, bathes his clubbed face in ditch water, and soon returns to the house where the Joads are sleeping. Ma welcomes him in the dark. He peels off his wet clothes, gets under a blanket, and shivers miserably through the night. His cheek is torn, and his nose is broken.

At dawn, Ma quietly gets up, quickly dresses, sends Pa for a little food, and then sees Tom's condition. She rushes over, and soon Tom assembles the whole family, including Ruthie and Winfield, and reveals the whole story. Al wants to get out. Tom tells him that he must stay. "Can't help it, Al. It's your folks. You can help 'em. I'm a danger to 'em." Ma feeds her family, sends everyone out to pick peaches, and hides Tom. When she learns of Casy's last words, she wishes that Grampa might have heard them and also forgives Tom for his violence. But she deplores the fact that the family is breaking up. Ma goes out to pick fruit. When Rose of Sharon becomes hysterical, Tom forces her to be quiet. Outside, he hears the owners' men quoting a price of two and a half cents to some newcomers. The deputies have broken the strike.

Later, Ma returns, talks sharply to Rose of Sharon, and then tells Tom that the jokes are all gone from the workers, that everything is bitter and mean. Then some men carry Winfield in. Having eaten too many peaches, he is violently sick with diarrhea. The Joad men return, and Ma orders Pa out for milk to give Winfield. All the rest sit down to corn meal mush, sugar, and coffee. Ma sneaks a trifle of milk to Rose of Sharon.

When Pa reveals that Tom's victim is dead, Ma determines to smuggle Tom off the ranch between mattresses on the truck bed. They load up, get a little gas with change from a work slip, tell the men at the gate that they have a steadier job back at Weedpatch, and then drive north instead for twenty miles or so along back roads until they happen to see a sign appealing for cotton pickers. Tom urges the family to hire on at the field. Meanwhile he will hide in a nearby weedy culvert until his face heals.

Commentary

This is the longest chapter in the entire novel, and the most decisive. It begins with the Joad family being forced out of the idle security of the government camp, and it ends with Tom on the run from the police for having committed murder. In between, Casy is brutally killed, Rose of Sharon seems to be turning irresponsible through worry and pain, Al starts to talk selfishly, and Pa loses his remaining authority over the family. Only Ma remains strong and un-

selfish. The background against which these personal tragedies are enacted is the larger tragedy of a strike broken by
the owners' vicious use of force and scab labor. The leading
figure in this larger tragedy, and the immolated victim in it,
is Jim Casy, who emerges as a Christ figure. Significantly,
Ma first perceives the import of Casy's last words, which
are close to those of Christ on the cross.

From the Critics

"The Joad family fled the Oklahoma Leviathan [the
bank], only to run into his brother, the California Leviathan
—the Farmers' Association and its typical member, the
Hooper ranch, a veritable prison with its barbed-wire fences
and armed guards—much the same sort of creature, but even
meaner." [54]

"Outside the tent where he [Casy] speaks, in a darkness like that on the Mount of Olives, are the California
deputies, twentieth-century versions of the Roman soldiers
lent to the High Priest, bent on destroying him. They catch
him finally in the hard beams of their flashlights, in the
midst of a stream which like the Jordan is a symbol of both
life and death, and he falls beneath their clubs echoing the
words of Christ on the Cross . . ." [55]

Chapter 27   Summary

Signs on the roads advertise for cotton pickers. Each
worker who needs a bag must buy one for a dollar. He gets
eighty cents per hundred pounds of cotton picked. If he fails
to keep a record each time he takes his sack to the weigher,

---

[54]Fontenrose, *Steinbeck,* p. 72.

[55]Crockett, "The Bible and *"The Grapes of Wrath,"* p. 196.

he is likely to be cheated. To balance the crooked scales, he puts a few rocks and clods into each load. One field which would have provided rather steady work for fifty pickers is swarmed over by five hundred, and the work is quickly ended. They tell the story of one man who never worked in a given area long enough to pay for his bag. By night-fall a whole family of pickers might have earned enough for a few pounds of side-meat. But the winter is coming.

Commentary

This short intercalary chapter forewarns us that the Joads will not be successful here either. The next chapter will present the beginning of the end for them.

Chapter 28   Summary

The Joads are living better now. They have half a box-car, which they share with a family named Wainwright. Tom is still in hiding. The rest are picking cotton steadily. Once, they drove to Tulare and bought a tin stove and some new overalls and a dress. Ma feels almost domestic again.

And then one day Ma buys Ruthie some Cracker Jack, and the girl teases some of her acquaintances by nibbling it and refusing to share any of it. A big girl hits her, and Ruthie counters by saying that her big brother will kill her enemy, who says that she too has a big brother. Ruthie blurts out that her brother is a killer in hiding nearby. Winfield tells Ma. "Oh! My dear sweet Lord Jesus asleep in a manger! What we goin' to do now?" Ma says. She will not "whup" Ruthie, who rushes at her and buries her face in Ma's capacious stomach.

Ma packs a little supper for Tom and then strides off to meet him at the culvert. She calls to him. They walk together to his cave-like hideout, and she tells him about Ruthie and soon persuades him that he must leave. In the darkness she feels his torn but mending face and crushed nose. She makes him take seven dollars that she has "squirreled."

Tom begins to talk the way Casy did, about how one person alone has only a piece of a soul which is useless unless it is united with other souls: ". . . I know now a fella ain't no good alone." Then he recites part of the Bible, again remembering Casy. He is now determined to help the workers unite, the way they did successfully in the government camp at Weedpatch. Mystically, Tom suggests that he may become the spirit of all deprived workers: "Then I'll be all aroun' in the dark. I'll be ever'where — wherever you look. Wherever they's a fight so hungry people can eat, I'll be there. Wherever they's a cop beatin' up a guy, I'll be there. . . ." Promising — "Sure" — to come back to them when the trouble has blown over, Tom takes her by the hand, leads her out of the cave, and tells her how to get back to the boxcars. They say goodbye quickly. Her eyes burning but dry, Ma walks back fast and heavily.

Back in the makeshift home, Ma talks courteously with Mr. Wainwright. She informs him that a farmer has just told her there is a little work on his small cotton farm a couple of miles up the road. The Joads and the Wainwrights plan to share this piece of luck. Then Wainwright broaches the embarrassing subject of his winsome daughter Aggie, aged fifteen, and Al Joad, who walk out together every night. The Wainwrights want no shame. Ma says that Pa will speak to Al, and if Pa does not, she will. Wainwright thanks her and goes to his side of the boxcar.

Ma notices that Pa and Uncle John are downcast. Uncle John says that he feels half asleep most of the time now. Pa says that he devotes all of his thoughts to the past, then adds, "Seems like our life's over an' done." Denying this, Ma reiterates her faith in the people: "We ain't gonna die out. People is goin' on—changin' a little, maybe, but goin' right on." Failure and even death only contribute to the people's progress.

Suddenly Al enters and blurts out that he and Aggie want to get married; further, that he wants to leave the family and find a garage job. Ma is glad but asks him to wait until spring, so that he can take care of their truck for a while longer. Then the Wainwrights come over, and they all share coffee, pancakes, and sugar, by way of celebrating the engagement of Al and Aggie. Meanwhile Rose of Sharon feeling worse, creeps into some brush by the stream and turns heavily onto her back.

Before dawn, Ma gets the family up. The Wainwrights drive with them to the twenty-acre cotton field, and all are picking by sun-up. But so many other migrant workers appear that the farm is picked clean of cotton before noon. As they start back to their boxcar, it begins to rain. Rose of Sharon, who went into the cotton field too, is suddenly very sick. Home again, Ma takes charge, sends the others out to gather twigs, puts Rose of Sharon's feet in hot water, and soon has the family warm again, fed with coffee, and in dry clothes. The rain pounds down, dissolving the fibers of what little cotton remains unpicked in the whole area.

Commentary

In spite of a fairly happy beginning, this chapter describes the loss to the Joad family of Tom, who must come out of hiding and join the faceless army of discontented workers. His decision to live in the hole by the culvert is in marked contrast to his refusal (in Chapter 6) to enter the cave which Muley Graves offered to share with him. When Tom emerges from the California cave (which has a number of Freudian aspects), he is in a sense reborn and has become Casy reincarnated. Already he speaks like that martyr, and his avowed intention is to carry on Casy's work. The rain with which the chapter closes marks the end of the Joads' present way of life.

From the Critics

". . . Tom Joad . . . gradually reaches an understanding of Casy's message and takes up Casy's mission. . . . Tom Joad becomes the new Moses who will lead the oppressed people, succeeding Jim Casy, who had found One Big Soul in the hills, as Moses had found the Lord on Mount Horeb." [56]

"Ma Joad would be womanly and maternal in any station. If she had been a duchess, she would have labored with heroism for the integrity of the family and would have had a comprehensive vision of the serious social obligations of her class. The scene of her farewell to Tom . . . is of the pure essence of motherhood. The pathos is profound and free from a taint of sentimentality. The courage and devotion of the woman are sublime." [57]

"This last meeting between mother and son [Ma and Tom] takes place under conditions reminiscent of the prenatal state. The entrance to the cave is covered with black vines, and the interior is damp and completely dark, so that the contact of mother and son is actually physical rather than visual; she gives him food. When Tom comes out of

---

[56]Fontenrose, *Steinbeck,* pp. 70, 78.

[57]Lincoln R. Gibbs, "John Steinbeck, Moralist," *The Antioch Review,* II (Summer, 1942), 184.

the cave after announcing his conversion, it is as though he were reborn." [58]

"Tom's goodbye to his mother has in it some of the home-grown mysticism which I find annoying wherever it turns up in Steinbeck, but there is no getting around the fact that it also has an emotional tension to which the reader's emotions respond; there is warmth in these words."[59]

"That doctrine [of the Over-Soul] . . . is the philosophical basis for the famous speech that Tom Joad makes to his mother after Casy has been killed—those words which rang bravely and beautifully in 1939 but which, if you will forgive me, seem to have lost a little of their glow since. . . . What does get lost amidst the genuinely lyrical flow of that passage and in its infectious hopefulness is the element on which not only the social struggle but the art of narrative depend—the image of the sharply outlined, resolutely differentiated, concrete individual personality." [60]

"His famous farewell to Ma Joad makes it clear that he [Tom] represents not just the determination of the proletariat to organize and rebel against injustice, but a more universal and lasting humanitarian force, an aspect of the spirit of man which—the novel suggests—is found especially in the very humble when they band together in sympathy and mutual protection. . . . Eloquence of this sort, tugging as it is to be released from its realistic basis, comes perilously close to bathos, but in its tension-heightened context it protects itself surprisingly well." [61]

[58] Lisca, *Wide World of Steinbeck,* pp. 173-174.

[59] W. M. Frohock, *The Novel of Violence in America,* 2nd ed., rev. (Dallas, Texas: Southern Methodist University Press, 1957), p. 139.

[60] R. W. B. Lewis, "John Steinbeck: The Fitful Daemon," in *The Young Rebel in American Literature,* ed. Carl Bode (New York: Praeger, 1960), pp. 138, 139.

[61] Watt, *Steinbeck,* pp. 71, 72.

Chapter 29   Summary

Over the mountains and valleys of California the dark clouds march. Then the rain pours down. The water gathers into torrential streams. The migrant workers huddle together fearfully. Those who try to leave cannot get far, because the rain and mud stall their cars. There is no more work. The men go to relief offices but are turned away because of their insufficient residence in the state. Hunger and sickness run rampant. At first the native citizens pity the begging migrants. Then they grow angry at them. Finally they are afraid of them. Sheriffs swear in more deputies. In turn the migrants grow angry and begin to steal and to send their sons out to steal. Frantic men steal squawking chickens and do not even run when shot at. When the rain stops, gray skies spread over a wilderness of sodden land. The women watch the men and are relieved at the anger they see: ". . . the break would never come as long as fear could turn to wrath." Gradually the earth is lighted by pale green grass.

Commentary

This last intercalary chapter ambivalently contains both despair and hope. The rain terrifies the unemployed migrants and kills many of them. But at the end the "tiny points of grass [which] came through the earth" symbolize a Whitmanesque resurrection, and Steinbeck thus implies that the people, in whom Ma has abiding faith, will go on. This chapter helps unify the novel by connecting with Chapter 1, in which the women watch the men and are relieved to see that they do not break. But, although the people survive, some individuals do not. So we cannot assume now—nor, surely can we at the close of the final chapter—that all of the Joads will escape the busy coroners' wagons.

Chapter 30   Summary

Al takes the tarpaulin which has been used to curtain the Joads from the Wainwrights and covers the mired car with it. The two families are now one. The water continues to rise about the boxcar.

Pa suggests that a number of men throw up a dike to stop the place from flooding. They go out and try. Meanwhile Rose of Sharon, feverish and with a cold, feels labor pains beginning. Ma and Mrs. Wainwright walk the frightened girl and encourage her, while Ruthie, Winfield, and Aggie Wainwright are sent away to wait and hope for a peek. Rose of Sharon's screams pierce the area, and the men work hard at their mud bank, which holds until an uprooted tree suddenly ruins it. Al tries to start the car, but the battery is fouled and the motor is full of water. Uncle John is deeply discouraged. Pa climbs back into the fetid boxcar, and Ma shows him their daughter's baby—a blue little mummy of a thing, shriveled and stillborn.

While Mrs. Wainwright persuades Ma to rest and Pa goes out to buy some bacon and bread, Uncle John takes Rose of Sharon's dead baby and instead of burying it floats it in an apple box down the swirling waters, shouting fiercely, "Go down an' tell 'em. Go down in the street an' rot an' tell 'em that way." With the sides of the truck, Al builds a platform in the boxcar on which to pile the family mattresses and other belongings above the rising water. They wrench the boxcar door off and lie high on it and on the piled mattresses. Rose of Sharon wonderingly whispers something to Ma about her breasts. Ma feels the girl and nods in understanding.

Next day Pa splashes out and returns with ten potatoes. The following morning Ma angrily orders the family to get out. Pa reluctantly agrees. Al refuses, stays in the boxcar with Aggie, and promises to watch their belongings. Pa carries

Rose of Sharon out through the high water. Uncle John carries Ruthie. And Ma carries Winfield. They churn their way to the road and walk through more rain from darkened skies. Ma sees a barn on a slight hill. They make for it. Ruthie and Winfield play with a lone geranium on the way. Pa has to carry Rose of Sharon all the way to the barn.

Once inside, they see a starving man of about fifty and his little boy, who explains that for several days his father gave him their remnants of food and went hungry himself. They give Rose of Sharon a dirty but dry comfort. The man whispers something to Ma, evidently a plea that she care for his boy. She promises. The boy says that his father stole some bread and ate it, but was so sick that he immediately vomited. Suddenly the boy screams that his father is dying.

Pa and Uncle John stand by, helplessly. Ma suddenly looks at Rose of Sharon, who looks straight back at her. The girl catches her breath, smiles, and says, "Yes." Ma smiles. Rose of Sharon asks everyone to leave. Then she painfully walks to the dying man and lies beside him. Although his frightened eyes protest af first, she gives him her breast. "You got to," she says and, putting her hand behind his head, mysteriously smiles.

Commentary

In this final chapter, the Joads are pictured as desperate because of man's inhumanity to man and also because of a seemingly malevolent nature. Pa rises to the occasion and tries unsuccessfully to build a dike against the flood. Ma twice voices Casy's philosophy when she says, "We'll do what we got to do," and "Use' ta be the fambly was fust. It ain't so now. It's anybody." Even Mrs. Wainwright, who never met Casy, echoes him when she answers Pa's complaint that it would be against the law to bury the dead baby privately: "They's lots a things 'gainst the law that we can't he'p doin'." (In Chapter 13 Casy said, "Law changes, . . . but 'got to's' go on.") Rose of Sharon is touched by her tragedy into an allegorical figure of compassion. In the last few chapters she complains less and less, and her final act of generosity to a stranger is a stunning conclusion best read as a symbolic affirmation of human interdependence. The novel opened with a description of the devastating dust storm. It closes with a flood. Steinbeck seems to be saying that it is enough for men to battle the elements, that they should close ranks in that struggle and help one another.

From the Critics

"These parallels to the Israelites of Exodus are all brought into focus when, near the end, Uncle John sets Rose of Sharon's stillborn child in an old apple crate (like Moses in the basket), sets the box in a stream . . . , and floats it toward the town . . ." [62]

"Pa's learning the lesson of co-operation is shown in his action of building a dam to hold the flood-water out of the cotton-pickers' camp . . ." [63]

"In order to gain time for the birth of the baby, the men must organize themselves and build a dike against the flood. For a while their strenuous efforts prevail . . . At this point, we have reached a conceivable ending of the novel . . . we are in the presence of certain conventions deriving from proletarian fiction—so allow me to call this Steinbeck's 'proletarian' ending to *The Grapes of Wrath*." [64]

---

[62]Lisca, *Wide World of Steinbeck*, p. 170.

[63]French, *Steinbeck*, p. 106.

[64]Chametzky, "The Ambivalent Endings of *The Grapes of Wrath*," p. 41.

"No solution is reached in the book: the climactic incident of Rose of Sharon, having lost her own baby, suckling a starving stranger, indicates that Steinbeck finds his answer in love rather than in revolution." [65]

"It is true that in a sociological sense the novel is unfinished, because Steinbeck does not tell us whether the migrants survive or disappear. He did not, however, know what the outcome of their struggles would be when he wrote; and he was writing a literary allegory [of the Joads' emotional education] and not a sociological prophecy." [66]

"But the lack of an ending in any final sense is in keeping with the basic idea of the novel. The continued faith in the search, in spite of failure to find opportunity and justice, is . . . effective . . . In a way, the uncompleted journey toward opportunity and justice is parallel to the modern tragedy, which decrees life, not death, for its hero." [67]

"The much-discussed concluding scene is an error of judgment. . . . The trouble is that it strikes a false and sentimental note at the end of a novel which up to that point has existed in an emotional medium as pure and affecting as any in our literature." [68]

"The conclusion is consciously sensational, to the embarrassment of readers of delicate sensibility and a strong sense of decorum. But Steinbeck's intention is clear: he wanted to end with a powerful symbol of human life persisting despite the hostility of social forms and of nature . . ." [69]

---

[65]Walcutt, *American Literary Naturalism*, p. 263.

[66]French, *Steinbeck*, p. 100.

[67]B. R. McElderry, Jr., *"The Grapes of Wrath:* In the Light of Modern Critical Theory," *College English*, V (March, 1944), 311.

[68]Bernard DeVoto, "American Novels: 1939," *Atlantic Monthly*, CLXV (January, 1940), 68.

[69]Watt, *Steinbeck*, p. 74.

"Some readers have objected to the closing scene . . . The episode not only has folkloristic and literary antecedents, . . . but for Steinbeck it is an oracular image, forecasting in a moment of defeat and despair the final triumph of the people—a contingent forecast, for only if the people nourish and sustain one another will they achieve their ends. More than that, the episode represents the novel's most comprehensive thesis, that all life is one and holy, and that every man, in Casy's words, 'jus' got a little piece of a great big soul.' " [70]

"Steinbeck ends his book on a quiet note: that life can go on, and that people can and must succour one another. If this is an 'evasion' of some of the social, political, and ideological directions in the novel, then I suggest that it is an honest, honorable, and even prophetic one." [71]

"Whereas earth has grown unproductive, the people have not, and Rose of Sharon's pregnancy, a living symbol of hope and immortality, becomes progressively more important to a complete understanding of what Steinbeck is doing. . . . Then why is the infant stillborn? . . . It is as if the human sacrifice of Rose of Sharon's baby has removed the curse of sterility from the cosmos. The baby dies as the result of *past* occurrences. But if Chapter One was all drought and despair, Chapter Thirty is all water and hope, on a super-Joad level." [72]

"At the end of the book the new collective organism is still in its infancy. This is the child that has been born, not Rose of Sharon's that was conceived of the selfish Connie Rivers; and her final act symbolizes this truth. It is a ritual

[70]Fontenrose, *Steinbeck,* p. 69.

[71]Chametzky, "The Ambivalent Endings of *The Grapes of Wrath,*" p. 44.

[72]Pollock, "On the Ending of 'The Grapes of Wrath,' " p. 178.

act: she who cannot be mother of a family adopts the newly born collective person as represented by one of 'the people [who] sat huddled together' in the barns when winter storms came. It is the family unity and strength imparted to the larger unit. In primitive adoption rituals the adopting mother offers her breast to the adopted child." [73]

"Then the miracle happens. As Rose of Sharon offers her breast to the old man . . . the novel's two counterthemes [increasing despair and increasing cooperation] are brought together in a symbolic paradox. Out of her own need she gives life; out of the profoundest depth of despair comes the greatest assertion of faith." [74]

"As the Joads hover in the one dry place in their world —a barn—the Bible's three major symbols of a purified order are suggested: the Old Testament deluge, the New Testament stable, and the continuing ritual of communion. In the fusion of the three, the novel's mythic background, ideological progression, and modern setting are brought together: Mt. Ararat, Bethelem, and California are collapsed into a single unit of time, and life is affirmed in a massive symbol of regeneration." [75]

---

[73]Fontenrose, *Steinbeck*, p. 74.

[74]Lisca, *Wide World of Steinbeck*, p. 177.

[75]J. Paul Hunter, "Steinbeck's Wine of Affirmation in *The Grapes of Wrath*," in *Essays in Modern American Literature*, ed. Richard E. Langford, *et. al.*, Stetson Studies in the Humanities Number One (Deland, Florida: Stetson University Press, 1963), pp. 88-89.

THE GRAPES OF WRATH:

The Intercalary Chapters

THE INTERCALARY CHAPTERS provide a wide historical background and give statements concerning the economics behind the migration of Oklahomans and other workers, their plight as they set out and also along the arduous highway, conditions in California, and finally the clash of men there and the apparent hostility of nature there. The sixteen interchapters, which comprise one-sixth of the total number of pages, operate something like similar chapters in *Moby Dick* by Herman Melville, *War and Peace* by Leo Tolstoy, and *U.S.A.* by John Dos Passos, to provide a substantial basis of assumed fact and in addition an almost continental unity. The individual intercalary chapters have to do with the following topics:

CHAPTER	1	the dust storms of Oklahoma
CHAPTER	3	the unstoppable land turtle, which heads southwest with great determination
CHAPTER	5	the eviction of Oklahomans from their farm lands by the relentless tractors
CHAPTER	7	the used-car lots
CHAPTER	9	how the evicted farm families sell their unmovable property

THE INTERCALARY CHAPTERS

86

Main Characters

The Grapes of Wrath has a large array of characters. Some, like Mae and Al (the hamburger-stand owners), appear in only a single chapter and they are left behind as the Joads move on. Some, like the used-car salesman and the one-eyed man, are not even named. The following (in alphabetical order) are most of the characters in the novel with speaking roles or with names. The ones with asterisks (*) are the most important characters. The figures in brackets after each person's name or identifying description refer to chapter numbers in which he appears.

Al [15]

Al and Mae run a small hamburger stand on Highway 66. Although the Joads are not described as stopping there, an impoverished Okie family does stop to buy bread. When Mae is reluctant to sell them a fifteen-cent loaf for a dime, Al curtly and profanely orders her to do so. Al and Mae, who have relatively little themselves, instinctively want to help those even less fortunate than they themselves and also are united in their loathing of the pampered rich who stop for food and complain.

Black Hat   [24]

A disgruntled migrant worker in the government camp at Weedpatch, California. He and Pa Joad come to realize that if one is willing to take for twenty cents an hour a job that the other has been doing for twenty-five cents an hour, then ultimately neither worker will be safe and the employer will win. Black Hat theorizes that the migrants should organize and present a show of armed strength to the California landowners.

Bullitt, Jessie (Mrs.)   [22]

The chairman of the welcoming committee at the government camp at Weedpatch. Mrs. Bullitt, together with Mrs. Annie Littlefield and Mrs. Ella Summers, calls on Ma the morning after the Joads arrive. She is officious but kind.

* Casy, Jim   [4, 6, 8, 10, 13, 16, 18, 20, 26]

Jim Casy is the most important character in the novel who is not a Joad, and he is more important than any Joad except Ma and Tom. Before the beginning of the story, Casy was an itinerant preacher. However, beset by a notion of his own sinfulness (and with good reason), he quit preaching, went into the wilderness to think, and then returned with a half-evolved Emersonian philosophy (not theology) of brotherhood and social action. There is something of the mystic in Casy, who makes an initially reluctant disciple out of Tom Joad when he suggests to him that even if one person dies, those whom he has influenced keep him alive by carrying on in his footsteps. Casy's language is often quite crude, and his ethical relativism (approaching ethical nihilism) is disquieting. But in his struggle to articulate the sense of universal love he feels within himself, he is most moving. His death at the hands of enemies who know not what they do makes him partially a Christ figure (note that his initials are J.C.). Casy puts into common words the social message of the novel. Ma feels it. And then Tom acts it.

Davis   [5]

The driver of the tractor which cuts up the Oklahoma tenant-farmers' land and knocks over their houses.

Eaton, Willie   [24, 26]

The gangling, tough Texan who is chairman of the entertainment committee for the Weedpatch camp dance. His supervisor, Ezra Huston, is rightly suspicious that Willie wants bloodshed when they learn that the deputies intend to raid the camp.

Feeley, Willy   [6]

A deputy sheriff who, according to Muley Graves, is persecuting him. Muley hides from Willy in the cotton fields.

Graves, Muley   [6, 10]

The Oklahoma farmer whose property was near the Joads' and who mulishly refuses to be driven off by dust, tractors, or prowling deputies. His family has all gone west. He is reduced to a state little better than that of a hunted animal. He is almost demented. But we have a feeling that he will develop cunning and survive for a while.

Huston, Ezra   [24, 26]

The elected chairman of the central committee of the Weedpatch camp. He is tall and lean and dark, with blade-like eyes. He is a quiet, natural leader, and he restrains Willie Eaton and Jule Vitela, thus preventing the authorities from having an excuse to destroy the camp.

Jackson   [24]

A supposed friend of the three would-be trouble-makers who crash the Weedpatch camp dance. Jackson denies having invited the trio, who are therefore quietly ousted.

* **Joad, Al**   [8, 10, 13, 16, 18, 20, 22, 24, 26, 28, 30]

The sixteen-year-old son of Pa and Ma Joad. He admires and sometimes imitates his older brother Tom and is something of a car mechanic. In fact, he loves only cars and girls, and frequently goes off "tom-cattin'." Although Al is proud to drive the family Hudson west, he is anxious to break away from the family and seek employment in a garage. He is likable but less responsible than Tom. Al has a chip on his shoulder and resents—but perhaps profits by—Tom's advice to stop imagining opposition. At the end, he leaves the other Joads and stays with Aggie Wainwright, whom he wants to marry.

* **Joad, Grampa (William James Joad, "Will")**   [8, 10, 13]

The honorary head of the Joad family, Grampa is an earthy, vulgar, cantankerous old man, who likes to brag about his former escapades and to argue about religion with

Granma. Steinbeck portrays Grampa with Chaucerian relish. He used to laugh so heartily that he would throw his right hip out of joint. He fumbles with his pants, scratches, has a foul tongue, and says that he wants to go to California in order to sit in grapes and mash them juicily all over his face and chin. But when the time comes to leave Oklahoma, he refuses to go and has to be doped with soothing syrup and piled unconscious onto the truck. Once uprooted from his ancestral land, he soon dies and must be buried by his impoverished family in a field beside the road west of Oklahoma City.

* Joad, Granma   [8, 10, 13, 16, 18]

Granma has a fierce, vulgar religiosity which is almost lecherous. She earned Grampa's everlasting respect once by getting a shotgun and nearly tearing off his buttocks with buckshot. Not long after her husband's death, Granma lapses into a restless delirium. She survives only until the Joads get into eastern California and then dies miserably at night in the truck beside Ma. Because the Joads have almost no money at that time, they must take Granma's body to the coroner for burial at public expense.

Joad, Uncle John   [10, 13, 16, 18, 20, 22, 24, 26, 28, 30]

Pa Joad's fifty-year-old brother John is usually quiet and hard-working. Years ago, his pregnant wife asked him to get a doctor and he refused, on the grounds that she had probably just eaten too much. She died of a ruptured appendix, and ever since then Uncle John has felt guilty and has tried to make amends by surreptitious little acts of kindness to children. Occasionally his sense of sin overpowers him, and then he goes on violent binges with liquor and women. But they bring him no relief. Now he rarely speaks, never takes the lead, and usually works uncomplainingly.

* **Joad, Ma**   [8, 10, 13, 16, 18, 20, 22, 24, 26, 28, 30]

Ma and her son Tom are the two most important characters in the book. Ma is a tower of strength to her group, like Pilar in Hemingway's *For Whom the Bell Tolls* though less articulate. She is a kind of pagan earth mother, kind to her father-in-law and her mother-in-law, anxious to let her husband Pa lead the family but quickly assuming the reins when he lets them slip through weakness and lack of understanding, firm but sympathetic with her children, friendly with deserving strangers (for example, the Wilsons and then the Wainwrights) but fierce when her family is threatened (for example, by religious zealots). Her actions reveal that she feels the truth of Jim Casy's philosophical pronouncements about the universal holiness and decency of life. Ma holds her family together far longer than anyone else in the group could have done. She suffers intensely when she sees Grampa die, then Noah disappear, then Granma die, and then Tom obliged to hide and then go away. But she almost never reveals the degree of her misery. She knows that while she holds, the unit will hold—unless man's inhumanity to man and nature's indifference put pressure upon her which simply cannot be endured. She goads Pa into near frenzy, knowing that it will make him stronger. She threatens to slap Rose of Sharon at times, but when the poor, pregnant, abandoned girl needs comfort, Ma is there with it in full measure. She knows that she can rely on Tom, not Al. She lets Uncle John have money for one quick drunken spree, knowing that without it he might crack. She rarely speaks much, but she once expresses the great comprehensive moral of the novel: "If you're in trouble or hurt or need—go to poor people. They're the only ones that'll help—the only ones." (Steinbeck more subtly demonstrates this truth by dramatizing the points that ownership is achieved by grabbing and is kept by violence, and that one is less generous the more he owns.) Ma never makes a mistake; more, she mitigates the mistakes of others by unselfishness and heroism.

Joad, Noah   [8, 10, 13, 16, 18]

Noah is the oldest of the Joad children. He is tall, quiet, and slightly misshapen—since Pa was obliged to assist at his birth. He is almost a Zombie. Often he is physically present in a given chapter but does not speak. He is steady and seems reliable; but when the Joads arrive at the cool river which separates Arizona and California, Noah quietly tells Tom that he is going to stay right there and fish and sit in the sun. Tom cannot dissuade him, nor will Noah even say goodbye to his parents.

* Joad, Pa (Tom Joad, "Old Tom")   [8, 10, 13, 16 18, 20, 22, 24, 26, 28, 30]

Pa Joad is the titular head of the family, especially after his father, Grampa, dies. But since he has neither the understanding nor the strength that his wife Ma has, he reluctantly defers to her judgment time after time. Occasionally he voices ineffectual resentment of this necessity. Among the other Joad men, young Tom is more capable than he, and Al is more ingenious mechanically. Without Ma, Pa would disintegrate. His one independent effort in the novel, the attempt to build a dike against the flood waters, he significantly undertakes while Ma is busy helping

Rose of Sharon deliver her baby; and his effort ends in failure. Pa never seems to understand the social overtones of their situation. He does not at first want to take Casy along from Oklahoma to California, whereas Ma instinctively helps everyone, within her physical limits. But Pa is a good man, and his last observed act is touching: he carries his exhausted daughter Rose of Sharon through the whirling waters on his back.

Joad, Ruthie   [10, 13, 16, 18, 20, 22, 24, 26, 28, 30]

The younger Joad daughter, aged twelve. She and her younger brother Winfield are fun-loving, adaptable, likable, pugnacious children. They provide a touch of comic relief for the wretched family. Ruthie's perhaps inevitable public boast that her brother Tom is a killer precipitates his departure from the family.

* Joad, Tom ("Tommy")   [2, 4, 6, 8, 10, 13, 16, 18, 20, 22, 24, 26, 28]

Tom Joad is the hero of the novel, the central male character, the person with whom we probably most nearly identify. Ma is the warm heart of the book. Casy is the only one with a philosophical mind. By the end of the story, Tom has become a combination of his mother's sympathy and his friend Casy's thought. Tom then goes forth to put his love of mankind and his socio-political philosophy into action. He is thus the one whole person in the book. But it takes a long time for him to come to this position of importance. When we first see him, Tom is hitchhiking to his farm home near Sallisaw, in eastern Oklahoma, from the state prison at McAlester, where he has done time for manslaughter. He is hot-tempered and cruelly tough, but he also has a delightful if usually muted sense of humor and is tender to members of his family. He is self-centered at first, but half in spite of himself he listens to and remembers the anti-materialism, ethical relativism, and socialistic talk of his friend Casy. Tom is obviously Ma's favorite, and this fact makes only the more pathetic her attempts to restrain his natural violence —he hates policemen and anyone else who tends to push people around—and only the more poignant her final need to give him up. When the Joad family are stopped by the police near Bakersfield, Ma whispers conciliatory words to Tom and then commends him for not trying to fight the authorities. After he kills Casy's murderer and must therefore hide, Ma pathetically tries to feed and keep him. During his stay in the cave near the culvert, Tom mulls over Casy's words and later emerges reborn, almost Casy reincarnated. This change in Tom is symbolized by his smashed and hence altered face. We know enough about him to believe that he will become a nimble labor organizer in the lush valleys of California and that he will effectively fight to put Casy's message into action. Tom and his sister Rose of Sharon are the only characters in the novel who undergo change. Ma does not need to change, since she is virtually perfect from the beginning.

Joad, Winfield [10, 13, 16, 18, 20, 22, 24, 26, 28, 30]

The youngest of the Joads, aged ten. He and his sister Ruthie are fun-loving, adaptable, likable, pugnacious children. They provide a touch of comic relief for the wretched family. For example, when Winfield accidentally flushes the toilet in the government camp near Weedpatch, which Ruthie has been trying out, they both think that it is broken. Winfield's diarrhea from eating too many peaches in the Hooper orchard is a cause of grave concern to Ma.

Joe [7]

The evidently busy assistant of the used-car salesman, who is anxious for Joe to soften up more potential customers and then send them on in to him.

Joe [20]

The labor contractor who comes to the first Hooverville the Joads live in and asks for men to sign up to pick fruit in Tulare County. When Floyd Knowles argues with him about working terms, Joe calls a deputy named Mike into the discussion. Soon a fight begins.

Joyce, Mrs. [22]

A timid woman at the Weedpatch camp whose daughters have been sick and have therefore used a suspicious amount of toilet paper. Mrs. Jessie Bullitt gives her some kind advice.

Knowles, Floyd [20]

A young husband and father at the Hooverville outside Bakersfield. He came to California with his parents. But they drifted apart, and now he does not know where they are. (This circumstance perhaps foreshadows the probable state of the Joads after the end of the story.) He and Al Joad strike up an acquaintance while Floyd is grinding the valves on his ancient Buick. He later advises Tom Joad to act "bull-simple" if the deputies try to push him into an argument. But then he too intelligently quizzes a labor contractor named Joe, who then calls for help from a deputy named Mike. In the ensuing argument, Floyd slugs the deputy and runs away. As Mike is about to shoot at Floyd, Tom trips him and Casy kicks him into unconsciousness. This episode precipitates most of the remaining action.

Littlefield, Annie (Mrs.) [22]

One of the members of the welcoming committee at the government camp at Weedpatch, the chairwoman of which is Mrs. Jessie Bullitt and another member of which is Mrs. Ella Summers. The three call on Ma the morning after the Joads arrive.

Mae [15]

Mae and Al run a small hamburger stand on Highway 66. Although the Joads are not described as stopping here, an impoverished Okie family does stop to buy bread. When Mae is reluctant to sell them a fifteen-cent loaf for a dime, Al tells her to do so. Mae goes on and lets the bug-eyed Okie children have two pieces of nickel candy for a penny. Mae and Al, who have relatively little themselves, instinctively want to help those even less fortunate than they themselves and also are united in their loathing of the pampered rich who stop for food and complain. Mae calls them "shitheels" and much prefers truckers.

Mike [20]

The fat deputy whom the Tulare labor contractor named Joe calls in for muscular support. Mike tries to arrest Floyd Knowles, who slugs him and runs away. Tom Joad trips Mike as he is about to shoot at Floyd. Then Mike fires but hits a woman in the knuckles. Then Jim Casy kicks him in the neck and thus renders him unconscious. When Mike comes to, Casy takes all the blame and allows himself to be arrested.

One-eyed man   [16]

An employee at a junk-yard near Santa Rosa, New Mexico, to which Tom and Al Joad go in search of auto parts. When the one-eyed man whines out some complaints about his condition, Tom rudely but perhaps helpfully tells him off.

Proprietor of camp   [16]

The proprietor of a camp near Santa Rosa, New Mexico, where the Joads pay to stop. When Tom follows in the Wilsons' car, he objects to being charged in addition. Tom regards the proprietor as a parasite victimizing itinerant Okies moving west. This property owner stirs the latent and smouldering hatred of Tom.

Ragged man   [16]

This man is a prophetic voice of warning to the Joads. They meet him at a roadside camp near Santa Rosa, New Mexico, and hear him tell of unemployment and misery in California, which he has seen and in which he has buried his wife and children before starting to return home.

Rawley, Jim   [22, 26]

This merry-eyed little man with white, frayed clothes is the camp manager at Weedpatch. He is courteous, helpful, and able, but he has also been made gloomy by all the misery he has seen. His good manners when he first calls on Ma charm that initially suspicious woman.

Rivers, Connie   [10, 13, 16, 18, 20]

Rose of Sharon's lean, pale-eyed, nineteen-year-old husband. Connie accompanies the Joads on their trek west. He is never described as doing much of the work, and he often complains, since—he says—he wants to break away and learn to be a radio repairman. Rose of Sharon's hopes for a nice little house for their unborn baby are blasted by many circumstances, including Connie's desertion of the Joads shortly after they get to Bakersfield. When Connie is gone, Pa tells Rose of Sharon that he was no good. Tom later calls him a "snot-nose" but leaves word for him, just in case, when they depart from the Hooverville for the Weedpatch camp.

* Rivers, Rose of Sharon Joad ("Rosasharn")   [10, 13, 16, 18, 20, 22, 24, 26, 28, 30]

Rose of Sharon is Ma's and Pa's older daughter, Tom's sister, and Connie Rivers' wife, who is pregnant when we first meet her. Pa tells Tom vaguely that the baby is due in three or four or five months. Rose of Sharon's constantly increasing physical discomfort helps to mark the stages of the Joads' fortune. Before the novel starts, the girl changed from a wild, sensual hoyden to a self-centered girl concentrating upon the wonder of her own miraculous future. For much of the story, she takes every jolt of the truck and fate as a personal threat to her baby. After Connie leaves her, she is terribly miserable. When Tom's killing of the deputy threatens the family, Rose of Sharon seems to become momentarily insane and then stupidly passive. But just before the baby is due, she commendably goes into the cotton field near Tulare and though in agony picks alongside the other Joads. She faces childbirth bravely. After her baby is stillborn, a wrinkled blue mummy which never had a chance, Rose of Sharon in the most moving incident of the entire novel gives her breast to save a starving man. She and her brother Tom are the only characters in the novel who change. Ma does not need to change, since she is virtually perfect from the beginning.

Sandry, Lisbeth (Mrs.)   [22]

A religious zealot at the Weedpatch camp. When she terrifies Rose of Sharon by hinting that the girl may lose her baby as a punishment for sinful dances, Ma tells her to get out. Mrs. Sandry then throws a fit and begins to moan.

Summers, Ella (Mrs.)   [22]

One of the members of the welcoming committee at the government camp at Weedpatch, the chairman of which is Mrs. Jessie Bullitt and another member of which is Mrs. Annie Littlefield. The three call on Ma the morning after the Joads arrive.

Thomas, Mr.   [22]

The small rancher near Weedpatch for whom Timothy Wallace, his son Wilkie, and Tom Joad work for a few days laying pipe. Mr. Thomas apologetically reduces their pay from thirty cents an hour to twenty-five cents an hour in order to avoid trouble with the powerful Farmers' Association.

Used-car salesman   [7]

A typical used-car salesman of the time. He squeezes the last possible dollar out of the desperate Okies, who must have some means of transportation west if they are to escape the dust and starvation. He loads transmissions and gears with sawdust, offers next to nothing for good mules in trade, and uses vicious high-pressure tactics.

Vitela, Jule   [24, 26]

A half-Cherokee at the Weedpatch camp. With Tom, Jule stands guard at the gate before the dance begins, to keep out any potential´trouble-makers. He spots the three men who were paid by the police to stir up trouble and thus give them an excuse to destroy the camp. Ezra Huston, his supervisor, restrains blood-thirsty Jule from beating up the trio.

Wainwright, Aggie   [28, 30]

The fifteen-year-old girl with whom Al Joad has struck up an acquaintance in the cotton area near Tulare. She and her parents share a boxcar with the Joads. The Wainwrights' speaking to the Joads about this friendship and its possible shame to Aggie probably contributes to Al's later statement that the two are going to get married. After Rose of Sharon has her baby and the flood waters threaten the boxcar, Al decides to stay there with Aggie and guard the Joads' belongings.

Wainwright, Mr.   [28, 30]

Wainwright and his wife and daughter Aggie share a boxcar with the Joads near Tulare. The Wainwrights ride with the Joads to their last cotton-picking job before the rains ruin the fields and force them to leave the boxcar.

Wainwright, Mrs.   [28, 30]

Mrs. Wainwright and her husband and daughter Aggie share a boxcar with the Joads near Tulare. The Wainwrights ride with the Joads to their last cotton-picking job before the rains ruin the fields. Mrs. Wainwright assists Ma when Rose of Sharon has her baby.

Wallace, Timothy   [22]

A Weedpatch resident. He and his son Wilkie tell Tom Joad about the pipe-laying job at Mr. Thomas's ranch, and the three men work there happily for a few days.

Wallace, Wilkie   [22]

A Weedpatch resident. He and his father Timothy tell Tom Joad about the pipe-laying job at Mr. Thomas's ranch, and the three men work there happily for a few days. Wilkie is presumably married to the young mother in the Wallace tent.

Wallace, Mrs. Wilkie   [22]

This young mother in the Wallace tent at the Weedpatch camp is presumably married to Wilkie Wallace. She deftly cooks a breakfast of bacon and biscuits, which Tom smells greedily. At the same time she nonchalantly nurses her tiny baby. This girl's unembarrassed competence perhaps foreshadows Rose of Sharon's ultimate gesture of generosity.

Watchman [22]

This man welcomes the Joads to the government camp at Weedpatch and explains the most important rules and regulations.

Wilson, Ivy [13, 16, 18]

The Kansas owner of the broken-down Dodge which the Joads spot near a culvert just beyond Oklahoma City. Wilson and his sick wife Sairy are waiting there helplessly. The Joads stop and camp beside them. After the Wilsons help during Grampa's stroke and death, they join up with the Joads. Al and Tom repair the Dodge, which then can carry some of the passengers from the overloaded Hudson of the Joads. This cooperation is a simple symbol of human interdependence. The Joads must leave the Wilsons at the river dividing Arizona and California, since Sairy is too sick to continue. Ma forces Wilson to accept two dollars and some meat.

Wilson, Sairy [13, 16, 18]

Sairy and her husband Ivy Wilson are from Kansas and are trying to get to California in a dilapidated Dodge. When the Joads camp beside them outside Oklahoma City, she provides comfort when Grampa dies. Sairy has an almost divinely beautiful low voice. When the Joads and the Wilsons get to the California border, Sairy, who is dying of an unspecified malady, is too sick to proceed. She asks Casy to recite a prayer for her.

THE GRAPES OF WRATH:

Critical Analysis

The Grapes of Wrath is a great and enduring novel. Its structure, action, style and themes are matters which have fascinated general readers and professional critics ever since its spectacular appearance in 1939.

For the sake of simplicity, these topics will be taken up separately. However, the reader is naturally aware that in a work by a writer as subtle as Steinbeck, form, plot, manner, and message are all interwoven into one artistic fabric.

Structure

The Grapes of Wrath has an admirable symmetry. It is in thirty chapters. These thirty chapters fall into three main groups, each with its own locale. Chapters 1-11 take place in Oklahoma. They describe the geographical and economic conditions which have forced the Joads' and thousands of people like them, to abandon their homes and go west. Chapters 12-18 occur on Highway 66 and recount the terrifying trip of the Joads in their rickety Hudson. (Note that Henry Hudson was an explorer who also went west.) Fear, love, and death accompany the Joads. As they cross the beautiful river in Chapter 18, they are in a sense baptized for their new life in California. Then Chapters 19-30 take place in that promised land, which is finer than its inhabitants, who oppress the migrants and thus force them to unite. In the land which does not keep its promises, there is only one oasis of peace and security. That is the government camp at Weedpatch (a real place in California, south of Bakersfield). When the Joads arrive there, they feel like human beings again. But there is no work. So they leave and go to the Hooper ranch, where the homicidal clash between those who own and those who need is fated to occur.

Other symmetry is apparent. Exactly half-way through the novel (on pp. 309-310 of the 619-page book), Al stops the wheezing Hudson and points to the great, green valley spread out before the Joads like a land of milk and honey. They are ecstatic, awestruck. But the religious tone is immediately shattered. With her eyes on the fertile land below, Ma reports that Granma is dead. This is a climax in the book. Another is located in Chapter 26, which is the longest unit in the whole novel. In a sense this chapter is a microcosm of the entire narrative. It begins in the security of Weedpatch. But lack of income forces the Joads to uproot themselves from that temporary haven and migrate again. They drift toward violence. When Casy dies and Tom kills his murderer, there can be no more security for Tom. He must start to run. He begins to learn the truth of Casy's pronouncements on the Over-Soul, the truth that each person is a part of mankind. The entire novel is the story of the education of the other Joads also—especially Ma, Pa, and Rose of Sharon—as to this truth. Toward the end, as Warren French acutely notes, "Tom has . . . lost his clannishness and replaced it with the concept that one must give help to anyone who needs it. Gradually the family comes to share this concept." [1]

Giving the novel a contrapuntal unity are the intercalary chapters. The reader soon comes to expect the narrative line to be interrupted every once in a while so that the specific plight of the Joads can be placed in national and historical perspective. This technique has been criticized by many scholars, for example, Charles Child Walcutt, who writes that "The need for the interchapters . . . reveals that the author's acceptance of a transcendental idea has not carried over into significant form: the themes of quest and struggle [by the Joads] and the exposition [in the interchapters] of the capitalistic dilemma of scarcity and 'overproduction' are not structurally united." [2] But other critics compare the intercalary chapters to the narrative sound track of documentary movies, long and wide views in the movies, and the chorus in Greek drama, and regard them as masterful foreshadowing essays in themselves. [3] Warren French takes conventionally oriented critics to task as follows: "Steinbeck's method of interrupting his main narrative with material that does not add directly to the history of the Joad family especially upsets those who think a storyteller's duty is to get on with the story or those fanatics about 'organic form' who are neurotically indisposed against shifts in style and subject." [4] These chapters strengthen the unity of the book if one agrees that its purpose is to present the Joads as typical victims of nature and capitalistic society.

---

[1]French, *Steinbeck,* p. 106.

[2]Walcutt, *American Literary Naturalism,* p. 263.

[3]See Joseph Henry Jackson, "The Finest Book John Steinbeck Has Written," The New York *Herald Tribune Books,* April 16, 1939, p. 3; McElderry, *"The Grapes of Wrath:* In the Light of Modern Critical Theory," p. 311; Lisca, *Wide World of Steinbeck,* p. 156; and Fontenrose, *Steinbeck,* p. 69.

[4]French, *Steinbeck,* pp. 95-96.

An integral part of the structure of the novel is the intersecting tracks of decline and growth. Peter Lisca brilliantly demonstrates this pattern. The Joad family declines economically and in morale. They leave Oklahoma with some possessions, food, a car that runs, and health and hope. Gradually nature and society strip them of one thing after another, until at the end they have almost nothing and are practically without hope. But in a compensatory way, as they lose they gain: the Wilsons and the Wainwrights attach themselves to the diminishing Joads as surrogate family members; and as the Joad morale drops, Casy and then Tom develop a loyalty to more than family—that is, loyalty to mankind.[5]

Action

Chapter-by-chapter summaries have already presented in detail the plot of *The Grapes of Wrath*. So it has been seen that dust storms and the banks combine forces to drive the Joads west. The trip to California is deadly serious, and to many readers it is then that the novel is traditionally most exciting. The Hudson is the Joads' covered wagon, the hot desert is a staple of many "wagons west" romances, the troopers figure as latter-day Redskins, Ma takes over as a trailmaster when the going gets tough, and finally the survivors see the promised land.[6] Once in California, new miseries begin for the Joads.

If we regard Tom as the hero, the novel is the story of his initiation. He is a recognizable archetypal figure who

[5]See Lisca, *Wide World of Steinbeck*, pp. 171-174.

[6]See the provocative interpretation of *The Grapes of Wrath* as such a Westward-Ho romance in Bernard Bowron, "*The Grapes of Wrath:* A 'Wagons West' Romance," *The Colorado Quarterly*, III (Summer, 1954), 84-91.

crosses the threshold of the familiar, encounters challenges on his journey to the unknown land, proves his bravery during the encounter with the murderous deputies, and emerges as a people's hero. His helper is Casy, who lectures him, dies for a cause which he takes up, and is in a sense reborn in Tom. Like many a folk hero, Tom must turn his back upon the terrain of the familiar and even upon his own family, in order to accomplish what he is destined to do for the people. Ma senses the necessity of his mission, and so she bids him farewell with a kind of sober joy.

Once again, we must consider the interchapters. They contribute to the action by repeatedly giving us a large preview of specific Joad activity, which usually follows immediately. In time, the reader can be sure that when he reads in interchapters about the migrants' problems and activities, he will soon thereafter learn how the Joads encounter those same problems and become involved in those same activities. For example, in Chapter 23, which is intercalary, Steinbeck describes the music and the lovemaking in the migrants' temporary California camps. Chapter 24 features in detail the Saturday-night dance at Weedpatch at which Tom is a guard; and in Chapter 26 Al lightly says goodbye to an infuriated girl friend, and two chapters later he has picked up with Aggie Wainwright.

The controversial ending of the novel, during which Rose of Sharon gives her milk to a starving stranger, is the point at which various lines of action converge. Dust and poverty drove the Joads to California, which is now inundated by a flood of almost Biblical proportions. Their Mount Ararat is only a deserted barn; but it is a much-needed sanctuary, and their ark-like automobile is abandoned behind them. The Joads, especially Ma and Rose of Sharon, have learned that there is nothing special about their family except as it epitomizes all of mankind, which must stick together. And so Rose of Sharon's gesture, which has communion-like symbolic overtones, represents cooperation and hope growing out of poverty and despair.[7] Casy teaches Tom. The necessity of Tom's departure instructs Ma. Her courage and strength educate Rose of Sharon. If the novel were a proletarian tract, it might have ended with the men successfully building a dike against nature and surviving to strike against the selfish ranchers.[8] But it is instead, as Warren French shows, "a literary allegory" the purpose of which is to dramatize the stages of the Joads' education.[9]

Style

Steinbeck is such a roughneck that most readers simply cannot believe that he is the master of a dozen literary styles, running all the way from crudities (which include words like "shitheels") to incantatory prose having Biblical sonorousness. The crudity has to be there, because Steinbeck is writing realistically about unwashed primitives who have been brutalized by fierce nature and starvation wages. We can hardly expect intellectual sophistication from Tom, for example, when we are told that his memory of the Bible has become distorted since he read a second book — *The Winning of Barbara Worth* (Chapter 10).

The wonder is that Steinbeck can make his characters as appealing as they obviously are to varieties of readers. All of this is not to suggest that his figures lack stature. Casy is an impressive creation, and his struggle to verbalize his honestly achieved philosophical conclusions is poignant and credible. Too often a reader is likely to think that a literary

---

[7]See Lisca, *Wide World of Steinbeck,* p. 177; and Hunter, "Steinbeck's Wine of Affirmation in *The Grapes of Wrath,*" pp. 88-89.

[8]See Chametzky, "The Ambivalent Endings of *The Grapes of Wrath,*" p. 41.

[9]French, *Steinbeck,* pp. 100, 101.

character cannot be profound unless his diction is profound. Casy is a vivid disproof of this assertion. Although Steinbeck had to include low speech and unrefined conduct, the reader will be disappointed if he turns to *The Grapes of Wrath* in the hope of finding masses of obscenities and profanities. The facts of life are there, to be sure, but they are handled with the clean casualness of a farm report. The literary account of a typical family which nature and society try to brutalize must be brutally written. Surely Steinbeck's abundance of animal similes, metaphors, and symbols (for example, the land turtle of Chapter 3) owe their existence to his desire to link his people to the land.

Steinbeck is a master at recording human speech. Like Mark Twain and Sherwood Anderson, to name only two similar American writers, he lived among the people whose rhythmic talk he captures on paper. Okie talk is naturally the most prevalent, but in addition we have the cocksure staccato of the used-car salesman, the Kansas accents of the Wilsons, and the bullying measures of vicious California deputies.

Steinbeck's own voice is also varied. His prose in the narrative chapters is never crude, unless it is describing down-to-earth activities. When it is used to picture our vast land and its terrifying power, its wondrous fertility, and the indomitable life force of its people, the prose displays ingenious variety. As it does so, it becomes apparent that its most obvious sources and analogues are the Bible, Walt Whitman, John Dos Passos, and Carl Sandburg. *The Grapes of Wrath* is Steinbeck's Exodus and Psalms, "Song of Myself" and "Song of the Open Road," *U.S.A.,* and *The People, Yes.* The greatest stylistic virtuosity of all is spent on the interchapters. There Steinbeck is not hampered by the intellectual limitations of his Joads and Casy. There he can speak in his own voice, which has always been many voices.

To show the Biblical resonance of parts of Steinbeck's novel, Peter Lisca arranges the passage which describes the monstrous tractors (Chapter 5) in the form of lines from the Bible. In addition, he points out that Steinbeck uses grapes for their symbolic value exactly as in the Bible and makes of his Okies modern Israelites who leave their ancestral land and formulate new laws en route (as in Exodus and Deuteronomy).[10] Joseph Fontenrose follows Lisca's lead and suggests that the name Joad may come from that of Judah, that the hostility of Californians echoes that of the Canaanites, that Tom Joad's actions often parallel those of Moses, that Casy is the leader of twelve apostle-like Joads (including Connie Rivers, who is not really a Joad but a kind of Judas), but that Tom too is a Christ figure, and so on.[11]

Steinbeck is an expert at character delineation. The three main characters in his novel are Ma Joad, Tom Joad, and Jim Casy. Ma does not fundamentally change; instead, she only extends the scope of her loyalty to include mankind in general. When we first see her, Ma is the center of gravity of a compact family, the solar force holding the entire system together and radiating warmth and energy to its components. When Tom is released from prison, he instantly makes for home. When that home becomes a battered car, Ma again is its cohesive force, although Al and Tom have to do the driving. Ma can endure the deaths of Grampa and Granma and then the loss of Noah and Connie, so long as her favorite, Tom, remains near at hand. In their Cali-

---

[10]Lisca, *Wide World of Steinbeck,* pp. 161-162, 169-171.

[11]Fontenrose, *Steinbeck,* pp. 75-81. Finding Biblical overtones in *The Grapes of Wrath* started as early as 1956, with Martin Shockley's perceptive article "Christian Symbolism in *The Grapes of Wrath*," *College English,* XVIII (November, 1956), 87-90.

fornia "homes," he is her mainstay. Casy enters the Joad family simply to teach it the doctrine of the Over-Soul and self-reliant brotherly love, as translated into twentieth-century strike terms. The two most significant acts of his life are his painful enunciation of his social philosophy and then his dying to hallow it. The main disciple of this latter-day Christ figure is Tom. At the instant of Casy's death, Tom so acts as to be obliged to take up the martyr's cause and walk in his footsteps. Thus Tom experiences a rebirth, which necessitates his splitting off from his family. Ma's giving up Tom is the saddest moment of the novel, sadder even than the loss of Rose of Sharon's baby. But Ma gives him up to the larger family, the family of man. Paralleling Tom's moral growth is that of Rose of Sharon. At first she is self-centered and whining. Her loss of Connie, her immature husband, makes her understandably petulant. But just before her baby comes, Rose of Sharon forgets herself and works in the cotton field as hard as she can. After her baby is stillborn, her symbolic gesture of nourishing the sick man dramatizes simply but unforgettably what Casy has taught Tom and what Ma has learned upon bidding her son farewell.

Of course some of the characters cannot develop appreciably. Muley Graves, for example, remains stubbornly the same and hence will probably not long survive the changes sweeping over his land. (Note the almost blatant symbolism of his name.) The grandparents try to change but are too old and too firmly rooted in their homeland. So they die. Uncle John has been too badly hurt by life to remain free to change. So he can only continue regretting and dreaming of sin and drink. Noah is emotionally stunted from birth and hence withers away. Almost as much as Ruthie and Winfield, Al is too juvenile to care sufficiently for his family; but he does mature to a slight degree.

Minor characters are boldly sketched—for example, Sairy Wilson and Mr. Wainwright. We remember Sairy's musical voice, her stoicism, her consideration. And Aggie's worried father is the picture of dignity in distress. Steinbeck has the ability of Charles Dickens himself to set a casual figure before the reader's eye and fix it in his mind by capturing the tone of voice, the cast of thought, the significant gesture or act.

Themes

The Grapes of Wrath is typical of Steinbeck because it combines his adoration of the land, his simple hatred of corruption resulting from materialism, and his abiding faith in the common people. The novel opens with a gripping picture of nature on the rampage but also of strong men and women unbroken by it. Dust is trying to smother the life out of everything in Oklahoma. The novel closes in rain-sodden California, but the rain-battered survivors there note that green grass is tinging the weary land with a promise that life will continue. Between drought and flood, the Joads move through an impressive variety of scenes and weathers. Surely Steinbeck is suggesting that in a land possessing such dynamism the people ought to be able to help each other over local crises. If the people could only cooperate, the forces of nature might not seem so hostile, might even be harnessed for the betterment of all mankind.

But instead of cooperating, the people compete more fiercely than beasts. In fact, they create monstrous institutions — banks, land companies, big ranches, and canneries (symbolized by tractors, fences with fat guards, and the like) —which further destroy and dehumanize the individual. Steinbeck is careful to make his point clear. Each person is entitled to his possessions, but only so long as they are tangible and personally workable. When he gathers unto himself more than he needs, separates himself from the physical fact of his holdings, and owns through documents and exerts his weight through subordinates, then he is wrong. When too few people own too much, those who enjoy too little sustenance will unite under repression and fight to take what they need to survive. Ma Joad has little food to feed her own family, but she shares her little with her fellow "have-not's." When she learns of a cotton-picking job, she communicates that knowledge to the Wainwrights, with the effect that the Joads actually earn less money. On the other hand, big farmers and canners with already more than they need depress wages to realize greater profits and even dump produce and slaughter livestock to keep prices up. (It must be added at once that Steinbeck's brief presentation of the complex agricultural problems of the late 1930's is simple to the point of naivete.)

So Steinbeck places his faith in the little man and his instinctive ability to get together with others like himself for survival against the opposing forces of nature and the profit system. Steinbeck has Casy rephrase Emerson's concepts of the Over-Soul and self-reliance. Casy may be partly comic when he does so, but only because of his verbal ingenuousness. He is far better when it comes to active example. He helps unite the prisoners in the California jail when they effectively protest against the sour food there; and his death during the abortive strike at the Hooper ranch results in more determination on the part of those who survive him, including Tom. The Joads demonstrate Emersonian self-reliance when they nurse their spluttering truck and the Wilsons' car along Highway 66 to California. Casy the talker admits that he cannot repair broken connecting-rods, but Tom and Al can. And the common people can also dig graves, rig tents, grind valves, repair flats, find food where almost none exists, pick peaches and cotton, nurse babies and cook breakfast simultaneously, lay pipe underground, and so on. They relish work. They want neither organized psalm-singing nor organized hand-outs. They want to earn their food by sweating for it.

Give the common man a chance, Steinbeck seems to say, and there will be enough to go around. Like Jefferson, Whitman, and Sandburg, the author of *The Grapes of Wrath* trusts the people. Jefferson deplored federalism and advocated agrarian democracy. Whitman made a religion out of his worship of man *en masse*. Sandburg delighted in the little guy's endurance and G.I. know-how.[12] Some of this message seems anachronistic in the light of twentieth-century industrialism. But we must remember that Steinbeck is at his best when he is writing of the great outdoors, far from the mad city crowd. And if they need to do so, urban readers can surely translate his message into terms which make sense to them, just as we all must do with the message of Thoreau's *Walden*.

Place in Literature

If *The Grapes of Wrath* were simply a novel of social protest, it would now be as dead as Upton Sinclair's *Jungle* and Ida Tarbell's *History of the Standard Oil Company*. If it were as inartistic as most proletarian fiction of the 1930's, once-startling examples of which one can hardly even name today, it would certainly not continue to be the steady publishing success it is. Like Stephen Crane's *Red Badge of Courage,* which is about a specific war of a century ago but is also a parable of fear overcome and as such appeals universally to generations of readers, *The Grapes of Wrath* has an appeal which is timeless. It owed its inception to a

---

12See Frederic I. Carpenter, "The Philosophical Joads," *College English,* II (January, 1941), 315-325; and Chester E. Eisinger, "Jeffersonian Agrarianism in *The Grapes of Wrath," The University of Kansas City Review,* XIV (Winter, 1947), 149-154.

specific crisis which no longer plagues the nation. But in the process of dramatizing that problem and suggesting ways in which it should be combatted, John Steinbeck gave us a gripping novel with enduring characters and a message which is timeless. Ma Joad, Tom Joad, and Jim Casy—and in lesser ways the others as well—enact for us a story of the unending struggle of men of good will to make the promise of the land a living reality.

THE GRAPES OF WRATH:

Suggested Questions

and Topics for Review,

Discussion, and Papers

1. Discuss the symmetical form of *The Grapes of Wrath*. In what ways, if any, is the novel out of proportion?
2. Indicate the variety of scenes described in the novel. How does this variety enhance or strengthen Steinbeck's appeal? Is Steinbeck accurate in his description of specific locales?
3. What progress do the central characters make in the course of the novel?
4. Do you feel a sense of frustration when you meet and learn about certain minor characters, for example, Muley Graves and Mae, only to have Steinbeck drop them and never mention them again? Can you justify Steinbeck for this habitual procedure?
5. By means of what devices does Steinbeck vary the tempo of his action?
6. Identify and comment on the function of the Christian symbolism in the novel.

7. Is Steinbeck's use of symbolism effective?

8. What is Steinbeck's purpose in using Biblical parallels as he does? Do such parallels seem valid or far-fetched?

9. Defend Steinbeck against the charge that the interchapters are artistically weak and include thematic material which might better have been incorporated in the action of the Joads.

10. To what extent are the Joads responsible for their plight? What might they do to alleviate it which they do not do? Is Tom to be criticized for his impetuosity? Should the Joads have followed Connie Rivers and forced him to return to Rose of Sharon?

11. Is Steinbeck justified in portraying all California authorities as hostile and ruthless? Should he have created more sympathetic Californians like Mr. Thomas and Jim Rawley?

12. Do you believe that Steinbeck is candid when he pictures life in the migrants' temporary camps along the highway as generally peaceful and law-abiding? Should he perhaps included a fight, an assault on a young girl, or an instance of ostracizing? That is, you do feel that he is loading his dice in favor of the migrants and against the representatives of law and property?

13. Comment on Steinbeck's use of vulgar talk. Is its inclusion unwarrantable or justified?

14. Compare Steinbeck's handling of dialogue with that of Lowell, Twain, Cable, Stephen Crane, Sherwood Anderson, or any other American author usually regarded as also skillful in this regard.

15. Do you agree that Steinbeck's style is moving without being sentimental? Why or why not?

16. Take a relatively minor character, for example, Noah Joad or Floyd Knowles, and show how his omission might weaken the novel to some extent. Which if any minor characters might easily be dispensed with?

17. To what extent is *The Grapes of Wrath* a proletarian novel? naturalistic? realistic?

18. How might an avowed Communist criticize this novel? What if anything in it would he be likely to commend?

19. Compare and contrast this novel with a typical naturalistic novel, for example, *Sister Carrie* by Dreiser or *The Octopus* by Norris.

20. Comment on possible existentialist qualities in *The Grapes of Wrath*.

21. What Transcendental elements are there in Jim Casy's philosophy? Be specific.

22. How valid is it to call Jim Casy Emersonian?

23. How fruitful is it to consider Jim Casy a Christ figure?

24. Comment in detail on the controversial ending of the novel? Is it credible? Is it best read as symbolic? Does it violate the previous tone of the novel? Is it consistent with Rose of Sharon's previously demonstrated character?

25. What evidence, if any, does Steinbeck give us in the course of *The Grapes of Wrath* to enable us to guess at the probable future of the Joads? What do you think will happen to them? Will Connie Rivers return? Will Al make a successful marriage? What will happen to Tom? Will Ma and Pa survive? Is it aesthetically valid to ask such questions? Why or why not?

For Further Reading

Books and articles on John Steinbeck are very numerous. The following are suggested as being particularly illuminating:

Bluestone, George. *Novels into Film*. Baltimore: Johns Hopkins Press, 1957. Contains a perceptive comparison of the movie version of *The Grapes of Wrath* and the novel itself; also valuable for its own critical insights.

Beach, Joseph Warren. *American Fiction 1920-1940*. New York: Macmillan, 1941. Contains a notably early, two-chapter study of Steinbeck.

Bowron, Bernard. "*The Grapes of Wrath*: A 'Wagons West' Romance," *The Colorado Quarterly*, III (Summer, 1954), 84-91. Shows parallels between *The Grapes of Wrath* and traditional "wagons west" novels.

Brown, Deming. *Soviet Attitudes toward American Writing*. Princeton, New Jersey: Princeton University Press, 1962. Has seven pages devoted to Russian comments on *The Grapes of Wrath*.

Cannon, Gerard. "The Pauline Apostleship of Tom Joad," *College English*, XXIV (December, 1962), 222-224. Points out parallels between Tom Joad and St. Paul.

Carpenter, Frederic I. "The Philosophical Joads," *College English*, II (January, 1941), 315-325. A secular interpretation, showing that the philosophy in *The Grapes of Wrath* is a combination of Transcendentalism, Emersonian faith in the common man, and Protestant self-reliance; fails to treat Biblical allusions and Marxist political philosophy.

Chametzky, Jules. "The Ambivalent Endings of *The Grapes of Wrath*," *Modern Fiction Studies*, XI (Spring, 1965), 34-44. Down-to-earth comments on how Steinbeck's humanistic ending avoids both a New Deal and a proletarian-protest bias.

Crockett, H. Kelly. "The Bible and *The Grapes of Wrath*," *Col-

lege English, XXIV (December, 1962), 193-199. Many provocative insights, some rather far-fetched.

Dougherty, Charles T. "The Christ-Figure in *The Grapes of Wrath,*" *College English,* XXIV (December, 1962), 224-226. Sees Tom Joad, rather than Jim Casy, as the Christ figure in the novel.

Dunn, Thomas F. *"The Grapes of Wrath,"* *College English,* XXIV (April, 1963), 566-567. Aims to correct H. Kelly Crockett (which see, above) as to Biblical parallels.

Eisinger, Chester E. "Jeffersonian Agrarianism in *The Grapes of Wrath,*" *The University of Kansas City Review,* XIV (Autumn, 1947), 149-154. Discusses Jeffersonian agrarianism in Steinbeck and shows that in many ways it is anachronistic for our century.

Fontenrose, Joseph. *John Steinbeck: An Introduction and Interpretation.* New York: Barnes & Noble, 1963. A splendid introduction to Steinbeck; stresses his knowledge and use of the classics and the Bible.

French, Warren, ed. *A Companion to The Grapes of Wrath.* New York: Viking, 1963. To demonstrate the controversy aroused when *The Grapes of Wrath* first appeared, this research aid reprints documents from the 1930's and also critical material by Joseph Henry Jackson, Martin Staples Shockley, R. Orlova, George Bluestone, B. R. McElderry, Jr., Bernard Bowron, Warren French, and Theodore Pollock; it also includes *Their Blood Is Strong,* Steinbeck's 1938 pamphlet on the plight of the Okies.

French, Warren. *John Steinbeck.* New York: Twayne, 1961. A good general biographical and critical introduction; has a thorough bibliography.

Frohock, W. M. *The Novel of Violence in America,* 2nd ed., rev. Dallas, Texas: Southern Methodist University Press, 1957. Places Steinbeck in the tradition of "violent" American novelists.

Hunter, J. Paul. "Steinbeck's Wine of Affirmation in *The Grapes of Wrath,*" in *Essays in Modern American Literature,* ed. Richard E. Langford, *et al.,* Stetson Studies in the Humanities Number One (Deland, Florida: Stetson University Press, 1963). A recent superb essay on *The Grapes of Wrath* as art; stresses the theme of conversion and imagery deriving from the Bible.

"John Steinbeck Special Number," *Modern Fiction Studies,* XI (Spring, 1965), 3-103. Critical essays by Peter Lisca, Arthur F. Kinney, Howard Levant, Jules Chametzky, John Antico, Mordecai Marcus, Donna Gerstenberger, Warren French, Curtis L. Johnson, and James W. Tuttleton; includes an up-to-date, fourteen-page checklist of Steinbeck criticism, prepared by Maurice Beebe and Jackson R. Bryer.

Jones, Claude E. "Proletarian Writing and John Steinbeck," *Sewanee Review,* XLVIII (October, 1945), 445-456. Demonstrates that Steinbeck is not a Marxist.

Lisca, Peter. *The Wide World of John Steinbeck.* New Brunswick, New Jersey: Rutgers University Press, 1958. An indispensable pioneering study; stresses structural and stylistic problems of the fiction, builds sensibly upon the best of previous criticism, and includes much definitive biographical material.

McElderry, B. R., Jr. *"The Grapes of Wrath:* In the Light of Modern Critical Theory," *College English,* V (March, 1944), 308-313. A fine early essay on the artistry of *The Grapes of Wrath.*

Pollock, Theodore. "On the Ending of 'The Grapes of Wrath,' " *Modern Fiction Studies,* IV (Summer, 1958), 177-178. Discusses the novel's form and optimism.

Shockley, Martin. "Christian Symbolism in *The Grapes of Wrath,*" *College English,* XVIII (November, 1956), 87-90. Sees Casy as a Christ figure, because of his initials, his preaching, his going into the wilderness, his attitude toward those who kill him, and his death.

Taylor, Walter Fuller. *"The Grapes of Wrath* Reconsidered," *Mississippi Quarterly,* XII (Summer, 1959), 136-144. Competently criticizes *The Grapes of Wrath* from the point of view of traditional Christianity.

Tedlock, E. W., Jr., and C. V. Wicker, eds. *Steinbeck and His Critics: A Record of Twenty-Five Years.* Albuquerque, New

Mexico: University of New Mexico Press, 1957. An extremely useful collection, which contains a survey of criticism, a biographical essay, six pieces of critical commentary by Steinbeck, and twenty-two critical essays by Peter Lisca, Lewis Gannet, Burton Rascoe, Frederic I. Carpenter, Joseph Warren Beach, Lincoln R. Gibbs, Edwin Berry Burgum, John S. Kennedy, Freeman Champney, Stanley Edgar Hyman, Woodburn O. Ross, Frederick Bracher, Blake Nevius, Claude-Edmonde Magny, Martin Staples Shockley, Antonia Seixas, and Joseph Wood Krutch.

Walcutt, Charles Child. *American Literary Naturalism, A Divided Stream.* Minneapolis: University of Minnesota Press, 1956. Devotes part of a chapter, on later naturalists, to Steinbeck, showing his guarded optimism and his fine sense of form.

Watt, F. W. *John Steinbeck,* Writers & Critics Series No. 16. Edinburgh: Oliver & Boyd, 1962; New York: Grove, 1962. A well-balanced, brief interpretation by a British critic.

Wilson, Edmund. *The Boys in the Back Room: Notes on California Novelists.* San Francisco: Colt, 1941. In a chapter on Steinbeck, discusses the novelist's constant preoccupation with biology, including man as a biological specimen.

Barron's
Simplified Approach Series

The Simplified Approach Series is the key to real understanding and enjoyment of the greatest works of literature.

In a clear, easy style, the editor discusses the great writer as a person to know; tells why and how he was inspired to write as he did; explains customs and historical background to the work itself.

Then he gives a detailed, analytical summary of the work—spiced with direct quotes and allusions—to illustrate the actual style, content and meaning of the work being studied.

95¢ Each

A lively source of material for
discussion · book reports · term papers

ANDERSON:
___Winesburg, Ohio

AUSTEN:
___Pride and Prejudice

BRONTE:
___Wuthering Heights

BUTLER:
___Way of All Flesh

CHAUCER:
___The Canterbury Tales

CONRAD:
___Lord Jim

DANTE:
___The Divine Comedy

DICKENS:
___Bleak House
___David Copperfield
___A Tale of Two Cities

___DOSTOEVSKY

DREISER:
___An American Tragedy

ELIOT:
___Silas Marner

___FAULKNER

___FIELDING

FITZGERALD:
___The Great Gatsby

GOETHE:
___Faust

HARDY:
___The Return of the Native

HAWTHORNE:
___The Scarlet Letter

___HEMINGWAY

HOMER:
___The Iliad and
The Odyssey

HUGO:
___Les Miserables

___JAMES

___MANN

MAUGHAM:
___Of Human Bondage

MELVILLE:
___Moby Dick

___MILTON

___MOLIÈRE

___O'NEILL

___PLATO AND ARISTOTLE

___POE

___ROUSSEAU

SHAKESPEARE:
___As You Like It
___Hamlet
___Henry IV, Part 1
___Julius Caesar
___King Lear
___Macbeth
___The Merchant of Venice
___Othello
___Richard II
___Romeo and Juliet
___The Tempest

STEINBECK:
___The Grapes of Wrath

___Ten Greek Tragedies

THACKERAY:
___Vanity Fair

THOREAU:
___Walden

TOLSTOY:
___War and Peace

___TWAIN

___VERGIL

___VOLTAIRE

___WHITMAN

BARRON'S EDUCATIONAL SERIES, INC.
113 Crossways Park Drive, Woodbury, New York 11797